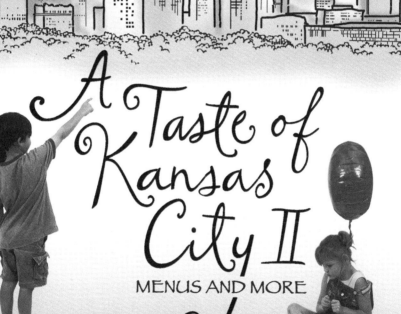

A Taste of Kansas City II

MENUS AND MORE

The Children's Center for the Visually Impaired

"A Taste of Kansas City . . . Menus and More"

3101 Main Street
Kansas City, Missouri 64111
816-841-CCVI
Fax: 816-753-7836
www.ccvi.org

First edition: October 2008

ISBN: 978-0-9727374-1-8

Table of Contents

A Taste of Kansas City II

I love food. Great, delicious food. When I'm not eating it I'm probably day-dreaming about it.

Stroud's incomparable fried chicken and French fries.

My wife's fantastic grilled pork loin and mashed potatoes.

The delicate tilapia and rich Caesar salad at McCormick and Schmick's.

The to-die-for pies hand-crafted by my pastry chef-daughter.

Ponak's Number 7 enchilada combination dinner.

My mom's pot roast and gravy.

I could go on and on about my favorite foods that instantly make my mouth water. I'm certain most (if not all) of you reading this right now could, as well.

I really like what Erma Bombeck once wrote about eating. "I'm not a glutton – I'm an explorer of food." That's me – an explorer of food. But I love exploring great food for much more than just how wonderful it tastes and how well it nourishes. Is there anything that binds us more as people, as families, as cultures than the love of great food – and the times we spend together sharing that food? Our holidays and special occasions almost always center on a feast – outstanding meals created by the tremendous cooks in our own families or the artistic chefs in restaurants the world over. It's universal and it's timeless. And in our hectic, busy 21st century lives, sitting down together for a meal has become extra special – a nurturing time as well as a nourishing time for families and friends. We laugh, we cry, we argue, we plan, we reminisce all around the table or the counter. We do business over food. We date over food. We get married over food and we celebrate births and graduations and religious milestones around food. And when we die, our loved ones and friends mourn us and remember us around food.

The creativity of food captivates us, as well. We revel in the preparation of outstanding cuisine. Over the centuries it's become a great art form, taking its place right alongside sculpture, painting, literature, film. In fact food often is a major subject of other art forms.

Talk of the great centers of fantastic food and your mind fixes on places like Paris, Tuscany, New York. But those of us who have spent any amount of time at all in the Heart of America know that Kansas City has a rich and impressive culinary tradition, too. Folks outside our area have heard all about Kansas City barbecue and beef. Those are powerful points of pride and fame for us. But Kansas City cuisine is much more than just barbecue and beef. My daughter, the chef, reminds me that our local food palate is as varied as the many intriguing cultures that make up our metro area. In our homes and in the thousands of local restaurants, bistros and diners, the traditional and unique appear on our plates to be savored and enjoyed and admired. Name a great food tradition from any country or region of the world and we almost certainly have it. Mexican. Italian. Thai. French. Chinese. On and on it goes. It's all here and it's wonderful. It's in the national and international chains and in the locally owned treasures, like the Kansas City Originals.

A discussion of Kansas City food wouldn't be complete without acknowledging the people who work hard and lovingly to grow and sell the luscious fresh produce that our outstanding restaurant chefs make a special effort to feature in their sumptuous meals and that we search for to put on our own tables. In spite of our extremes of weather that can give farm families fits raising delicate fruits and vegetables, the Kansas City region abounds with farm plots and orchards teeming with succulent produce. And we delight in weekly or even daily adventures to pick out the best of those gastronomical gems at just the right time of year in our local farmers markets, specialty groceries and full-service supermarkets devoted to freshness, quality and selection.

This cookbook brings to you a collection of the best of the traditional, the unique, the homegrown – the familiar and the recently discovered. In 2003, The Children's Center for the Visually Impaired (CCVI) scored big, putting out the first *A Taste of Kansas City / Then and Now*. It was enormously popular, far more successful than the most optimistic of the leaders of the cookbook project ever thought it could be. There are a lot of charity cookbooks out there but that little book had just the right recipe for success. Beautifully produced, it featured the delicious creative magic of the local food artists so many of us grew up with, weaving in fascinating background stories about the restaurants, the meals and the chefs. And it spotlighted the culinary wizardry of the new kitchen geniuses of our city. With its mix of the new, the unique and the traditional (and more than a pinch of nostalgia stirred in) the little cookbook that could has gone through six printings and 19,000 copies sold, carving out a place of honor and legend in the world of charity cookbooks.

But the recipe for success of that first cookbook had one other irresistible ingredient. It benefited a dynamic, well-respected local school that for more than a half century has been doing incredibly important and effective work educating our children who have severe visual impairments, preparing them to succeed in a sighted world. I've witnessed first-hand that miraculous work both as a news reporter covering CCVI's operations and as a volunteer, including seven years as a member of the Board of Directors. CCVI has touched my heart and I know it's touched the hearts of many of the people who bought the first *A Taste of Kansas City / Then and Now*.

It's time for a new one. People have been clamoring for it. Now you have it. There's just too much to love about food, especially Kansas City food, to limit it to just one cookbook, no matter how great it is. This new one has all that was extraordinary about the first one – and more. So dig in. Explore.

Phil Witt
Fox 4 News Anchor/Reporter
WDAF-TV

The Children's Center for the Visually Impaired

The Children's Center for the Visually Impaired (CCVI) offers a comprehensive program including specialized instruction, individualized therapy, consulting services and supportive family education. Founded in 1952 as the Kansas City Nursery School for the Blind, the first class had 13 students, eight visually impaired children and five sighted peers. Today, CCVI annually serves over 300 students and families through its Infant, Preschool, Outreach and Family Services programs.

Services can begin in infancy through the home based Infant Program and continue with Preschool and Kindergarten classes that prepare children for entry into the public or private school systems. Specialized services include braille instruction, orientation and mobility, deafblind services, assistive technology, low vision training, speech, occupational, physical and aquatic therapies and family support. In 1998, the Center moved to its current location at 3101 Main Street. While CCVI has seen many changes, one thing remains the same – wonderful community support!

The *Friends* of CCVI started in 1986. This seasoned auxiliary group has been going strong ever since, raising more than $2.4 million for CCVI! The group originated the Trolley Run, CCVI's largest annual fundraiser (originally the Michael Forbes Trolley Run, currently the Sabates Eye Centers Trolley Run). They've played a role in Holidays in Crestwood and have been the driving force behind the Evening in the... series of events. One of their greatest contributions was the creation of *A Taste of Kansas City / Then and Now*, a cookbook complete with dashes of history about Kansas City eating establishments. More than 19,000 copies of the book have been sold and it is consistently the top selling regional cookbook at Williams-Sonoma.

With the first cookbook now in its sixth printing, the *Friends* decided it was time for a new cookbook. Inside these pages are delicious recipes and tempting menus. You are sure to find dishes you will want to add to your list of favorites! CCVI is grateful to the *Friends* and its Cookbook Committee for mixing countless hours of preparation, cooking and tasting into this new cookbook-- all to benefit the Kansas City area's youngest blind and visually impaired children.

We hope you enjoy what is sure to become one of your most used and loved cookbooks. Thank you for supporting CCVI!

CCVI's Kids

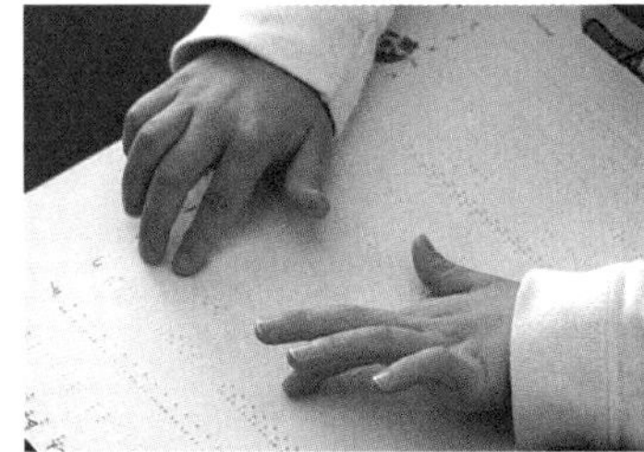

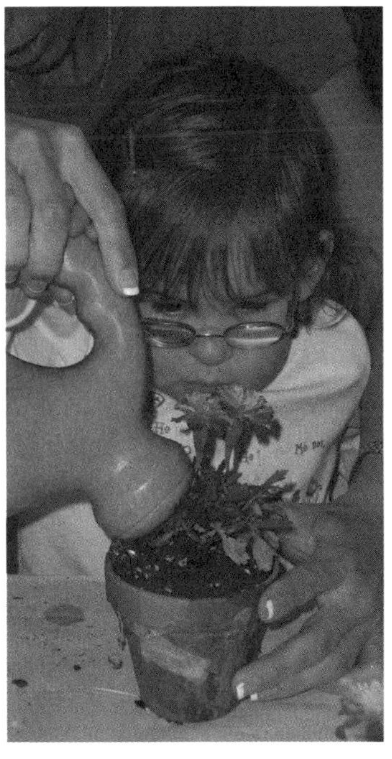

CCVI's Kids

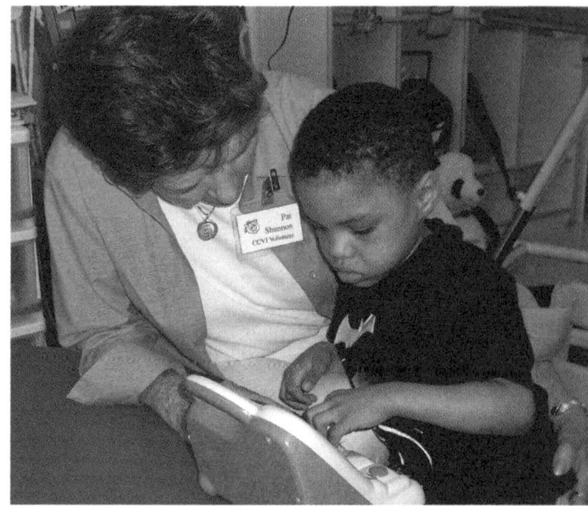

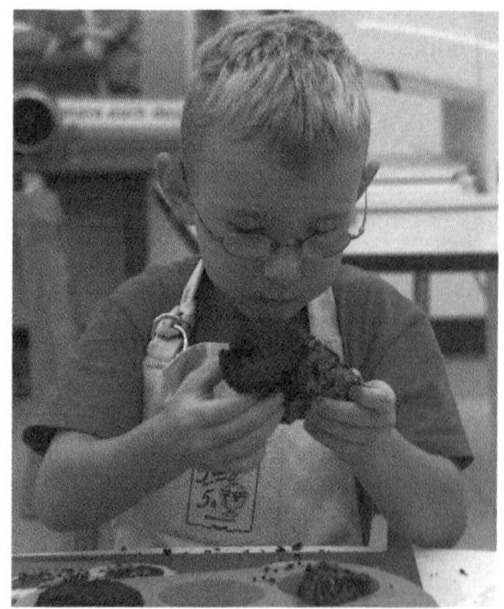

CCVI's Kids

Williams-Sonoma

The Friends of the Children's Center for the Visually Impaired

In the spring of 2007, the *Friends* of the Children's Center for the Visually Impaired (CCVI) observed its 20th anniversary. During a celebration gathering the conversation drifted to a discussion of the organization's accomplishments. It was during this conversation that the cookbook, *A Taste of Kansas City / Then and Now*, was discussed. To the surprise of many, it was revealed that the book, in its sixth printing, has netted over $170,000 for CCVI. Many stores, Kansas City events and individuals have helped in this endeavor. Indeed, the book is the best selling regional cookbook ever carried by Williams-Sonoma.

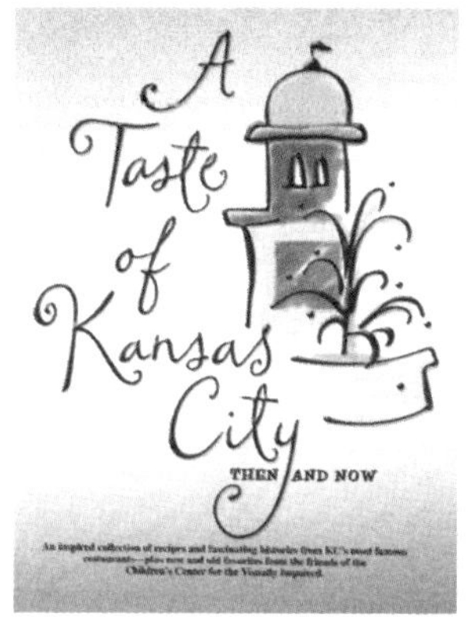

It is always difficult to follow a successful book, but we have given it our best effort. The call was issued to friends, chefs and caterers across the area for recipes and ideas and in they "poured." Most are from Kansas City, of course, but others came from Washington, D.C. to San Francisco and many points in between.

Testing and tasting groups were formed, including taste buds of all ages. Old friendships were renewed and new friendships formed. Surely a few pounds were gained by many of us while enjoying great food, with little discipline to limit our intake. Choosing recipes for a cookbook is always difficult. We have attempted to include a selection of new recipes and a few old favorites, flavored by a variety of culinary areas.

We have also embraced the idea of eating locally, and cooking with what is produced or grown near Kansas City. There are a number of movements that embrace this ideal, from Slow Food USA (an international organization dedicated to the pleasures of the table) to locavores, or people who try to eat what is produced within a 100-mile radius of their home. So, we sought help from area farmers who grow the delicious fresh foods frequently found in local markets, and many contributed to this book.

Numerous Kansas City chefs have restaurant menus that feature what is in season, and produced locally, as do many supermarkets. Further, many households purchase fresh produce from local growers; some even have it delivered weekly. We have made a concerted effort to include recipes that use these locally produced goods.

Thank you for helping support, through the purchase and use of this cookbook, a wonderful school that nurtures very special children.

Bon Appetit
Sally Cobb

Thank You to Our Sponsors

Gallon

Consentino Charity Foundation

Quart

Sally & Charley Cobb

Pint

Russell & Carolee Atha
Linda & Bob Cook

Cup

Diana & Jim Cusser
Jill Hall
Erma & Dale Peterson
BJ & Jerry Thornburg
Mary Jo Truog
Addie Ward

3/4 Cup

Tom and Susan Angulo
Larry Belger
In Memory of Barbara Darling Davis
Mr. John Lathrop
Bill & Barbara Koval Nelson
Jim Pittman-Black Tie Desserts & Catering

1/2 Cup

Arnold & Keck LLC/ Bob Arnold
Judy Curry
Jill & Marshall Dean
Mary Lynne Dolembo
Barbara Gattermeir
Kevin & Judy Glynn
Mike & Pam Goodmon
Pam & John Gyllenborg
Millie Irwig
Janet Kelley
Betty Klein
Larry & Betsy Piebenga
RT Salsman Catering, Inc.
Michael & Sunday Siragusa
Michele Stowers
Joan & Byron Thompson

(continued)

Thank You to Our Sponsors

1/4 Cup

David & Christina Bernstein
Jenny DeVry
Maria Burgen & Lottie Harris
Max & Patty Calliham
Chris & Jodi Cobb
Martha Best Dooley
Arthur J. Doyle
Matthew & Judith Deedy
Tom & Ann Duckett
Tom & Melody Gardner
Gary & Meg Grandcolas
Don & Carolyn Holder
Verna Hudson
Roger & Sandy Jackson
Joy & Jerry Kaplan
Janice McCollum
Nan McConnell
Jinny McCoy
John & Judy Miller
Sarah & Sean Murray
The Niemann Family
Linda & Tom Nocita
Lucinda Rice-Petrie
Kathleen Rapley
Greg & Phyllis Rick
Mary Jo Runyan
Monroe & Helen Taliaferro
Faye Werner
Gene and Mary Ann Wilson
Phil & Kim Witt

Other donors

Jo Hayes
Nancy Smith

Thank You

Special Thanks

Susan Belger Angulo
Baby Cakes in the River Market
Diane Barker
The Berry Patch
Casey Broker
Brookside Organic Farmers Market
Tom & Jennifer Coen
Charley Cobb
Cosentino's Food Stores
Mary Lynne Dolembo
Farm to Market Bread Co.
Carolyn Holder
Kansas City Farmers Market
Landeria Farm
Elizabeth Mayer
McGonigle's Food Store
Betsy Piebenga
Paul Mesner Puppets
Judy Miller
Traci Todd Murphy
Sally Pollock
Pryde's Old Westport
Red Cedar Country Gardens
Rooms That Bloom
Lindsay Rowe
Tammy Saam
Gene Schmidt
David & Sandy Spaw
Dana Stram
Beth Stone
Mary Ann Toohey
Williams-Sonoma
Victoria Wyrick

We regret the omission of any contributors.

Cosentino's

The Cosentino name has been associated with the grocery business in Kansas City since 1948.

Dante and Beatrice Cosentino raised their family of six in Northeast, Kansas City, and instilled values in their children that became the foundation for a successful family business that spans three generations.

Dante was the ecclesiastical painter for church interiors throughout the city and some of his murals remain today. He was in the Raytown area bidding on a project and stopped in at the local fruit market at 43rd and Blue Ridge to buy groceries and in speaking with the owner found out the market was for sale.

Dante thought the grocery business would be a good way for his children to earn a living and bought the store in 1948. Ten years later the building was razed to make way for what was called the "most modern supermarket in the Midwest." The 13,000 square foot Quik-Check Picture Window store was so popular that they had to close the doors on occasion when the number of shoppers reached the capacity limit. Sixty years later the store is still owned and operated by the family.

From the beginning, pleasing their customers was their top priority. They made available the best selection at the best price. The Cosentino's commitment to personalized customer service was at the core of their business and set a precedent that has become tradition.

Cosentino's Food Stores currently operates 23 stores in the Kansas City area. The first generation is proud to watch the third generation of Cosentino's family members now taking part in the day to day operations and management of the company.

Kansas City ~ thank you for helping to grow our organization. We take great pleasure in serving you!

Cosentino's Food Stores

The Children's Center for the Visually Impaired thanks Cosentino's for their continuing support.

Cosentino's Family Recipes

Homemade Granola

4 cups old-fashioned rolled oats
2 cups sweetened, shredded coconut
2 cups sliced almonds
1 1/2 cups dried cherries, chopped (or fruit of your choice)
1/2 cup vegetable oil
1/3 cup honey
2 teaspoons ground cinnamon

Preheat oven to 350 degrees. Toss oats, coconut, almonds and cherries together in a large bowl. Pour the vegetable oil and honey over the oat mixture. Add the cinnamon and stir with a spatula until oats and nuts are coated with liquids. Pour onto a sheet pan. Bake, stirring occasionally with a spatula, until mixture turns a nice even golden brown, about 25-30 minutes.

Remove granola from the oven and allow to cool, stirring occasionally. Store cooled granola in an airtight container.

Cake Balls

1 (18.25 ounce) package chocolate cake mix
1 (16 ounce) container prepared chocolate frosting
1 large bar chocolate flavored confectioners coating

Prepare the cake mix according to package directions using any of the recommended pan sizes. When cake is done, crumble while warm into a large bowl, and stir in the frosting until well blended.

Melt chocolate coating in a double boiler, or in a metal bowl over a pan of simmering water, stirring occasionally until smooth.

Use a melon baller or small scoop to form balls of the chocolate cake mixture.

Refrigerate the balls for about an hour.

Dip the balls in chocolate using a toothpick or fork to hold them. Place on waxed paper to set and refrigerate overnight.

Makes about 3 dozen

Other Flavor Possibilities

- White cake mix and mint chocolate chip icing dipped in chocolate coating
- French vanilla cake with white chocolate almond icing dipped in chocolate coating
- Red velvet with cream cheese icing and vanilla almond bark coating

Note: Confectioners coating is similar to almond bark but of a higher quality. It can be found in candy and confectionery supply stores such as The Sweet Supply Shop in Overland Park, KS. It is sold in varied amounts and flavors.

Buy Local

Tomatoes, spinach or berries – get 'em while they're fresh!

The more things change, the more they stay the same. In the past, mothers and grandmothers spent time in their gardens, gathering fruits and vegetables at the peak of freshness. Afternoons would often be spent snapping green beans or cleaning corn in preparation for that evening's dinner. Knowing the peak seasons for produce was second nature.

Then life became more hectic and people began turning to grocery stores to buy ingredients for their meals. Today, food travels an average of 1,300 miles from farm to table. According to the Food Routes Network, it can take some produce up to two weeks to reach its destination. What was fresh when it started the journey loses nutrients in that time.

However with current concerns about the environment and rising obesity rates, many people are once again hungry for seasonal, fresh, healthy food—food you'll find at local farmers' markets, supermarkets and through Community Supported Agriculture.

Look around a farmers' market, and you're bound to notice the variety. Why? Because the produce doesn't have far to travel. The City Market, located in the River Market area of Kansas City, was named the 2008 Farmers' Market of the Year by AgriMissouri and the Missouri Farmers' Market Association. What a great resource right in our own back yard.

Kansas City offers a plethora of local markets—north, south, east or west, there are growers offering food at the height of freshness. Downtown Kansas City, KC neighbor-

(continued on the next page)

Cal-Ann Farms

Buy Local *(continued)*

hoods like Brookside, Overland Park, Parkville, Liberty, Shawnee, Olathe, Independence, Lee's Summit and Merriam all have Farmers' Markets, offering shoppers the best of what's in season. Many grocery stores now feature "buy local" sections all year long.

There are a number of Community Supported Agriculture (CSA) programs in the area, too. CSA is a partnership between the growers and consumers. Usually, you can buy shares in a CSA farm, and you'll enjoy the bounty of fresh foods produced throughout the growing season. It might be meat, eggs, fruit or vegetables but one thing is for sure—the food will be fresh and packed full of nutrients.

Landeria Farm

Great meals start with fresh ingredients, and fresh ingredients are at your fingertips across Kansas City. Become a locavore, or someone who prefers to eat locally produced and grown food. Visit the following websites to find a market or CSA site near you.

Landeria Farm

http://agebb.missouri.edu/fmktdir/index.htm (Farmers' Market Directory, University of Missouri Extension)

http://www.oznet.ksu.edu/pr_kfmd/ (Kansas Farmers' Markets, K-State Research and Extension)

http://www.kcfoodcircle.org/ (Kansas City Food Circle—Connecting local eaters with local growers)

http://www.kcfoodcircle.org/KCCSAC/ (Kansas City CSA Coalition)

The Berry Patch

Beans
$6.00/lb

Home Grown
Blackberries
Butler, MO
4.00

The Berry Patch

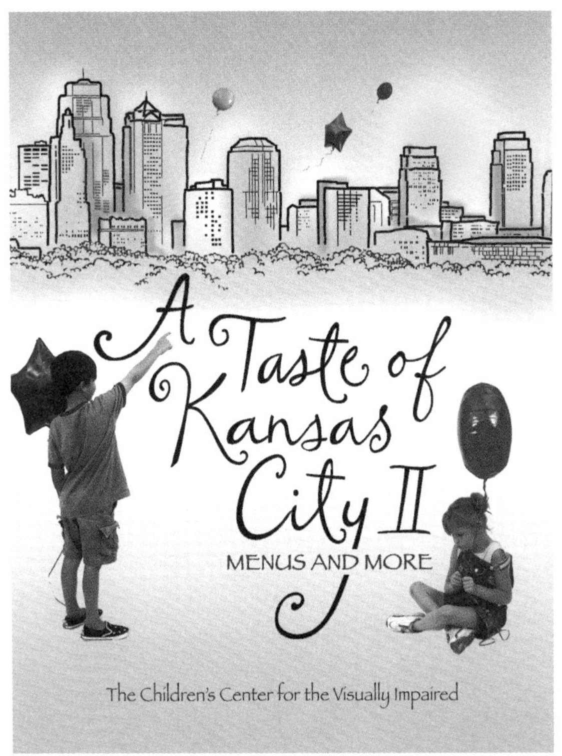

A Taste of Kansas City II
MENUS AND MORE
The Children's Center for the Visually Impaired

Table Settings and Menus

We hope you use and enjoy *A Taste of Kansas City II ... Menus and More*.

Several members of the local business world generously shared their beautiful table settings. They have suggested menus you'll find listed with the settings. All recipes are included in the body of the book. Use their ideas to make your meal a feast for the eyes as well as the stomach.

Additional menu ideas can be found on the title page of each section. They include recipes from this book as well as our first book, *A Taste of Kansas City / Then and Now*.

A Party with Paul Mesner's Puppets

www.paulmesnerpuppets.org

Spring Luncheon with Rooms That Bloom

Rooms That Bloom, 13442 Cherry, Martin City, MO 64145

Gazpacho. 55
or Chilled Corn Soup with Jalapeno
Crème Fraiche 56
Zucchini Salad with Red Onion 65
Ciabatta bread from Farm to Market Bakery
Panna Cotta 156
or Rhubarb and Strawberry Crisp. 140

Menu — Andrew Sloan, Room 39 at Mission Farms

Summer Menu in The Grape Arbor

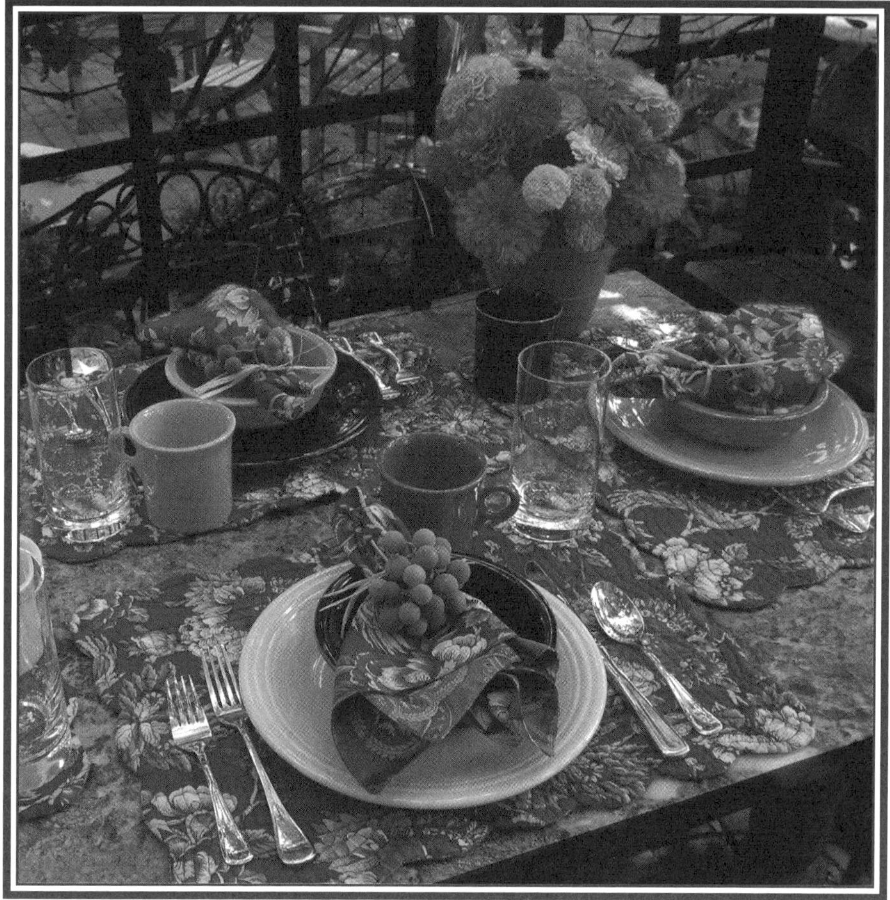

Tom and Jennifer's Grape Arbor – Table settings provided by Pryde's Old Westport

A Fall Menu from Pryde's Old Westport

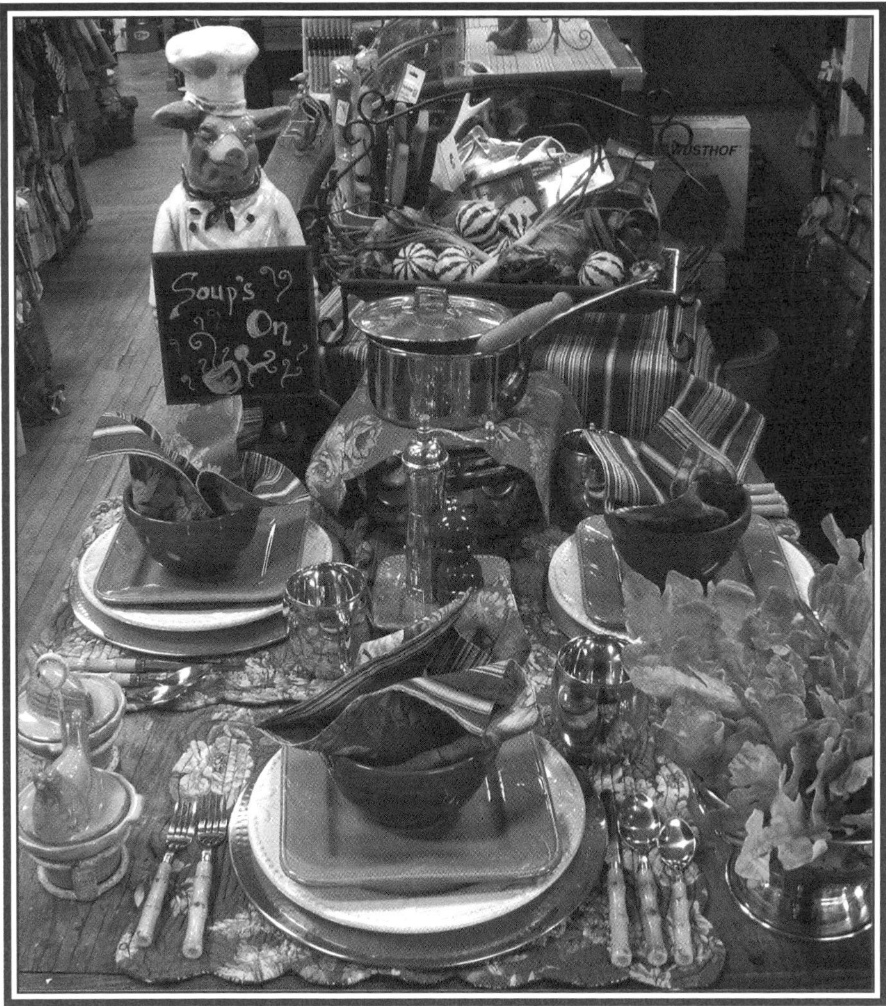

Pryde's Old Westport, 115 Westport Rd., Kansas City, MO. 64111

Winter Supper at Red Cedar Country Gardens

Red Cedar Country Gardens, 7895 W. 188 Rd. Street, Stilwell, KS 66085

Appetizers

Cocktail Buffet Menu Ideas

Appetizers

Grilled Shrimp on Rosemary Skewers

3 tablespoons freshly squeezed lemon juice
3 tablespoons extra-virgin olive oil
1 teaspoon lemon zest
2-3 basil leaves, torn into fine strips
2 garlic cloves, minced
1 1/2 pounds large shrimp, peeled and deveined
2 lemons
8 sturdy rosemary sprigs, each 6-8 inches long
Salt and freshly ground pepper

Whisk together lemon juice, olive oil, zest, basil and garlic. Add shrimp and stir to coat; cover and refrigerate 1-3 hours.

Preheat outdoor grill or broiler. Cut each lemon into six wedges. Remove any visible seeds, set aside. Strip leaves from rosemary sprigs, leaving a tuft at one end. Make a point of the stem opposite the tuft. Remove shrimp from marinade and season with salt and pepper. Skewer shrimp on sprig by passing point through both head and tail of each shrimp. Alternate shrimp with lemon on sprig. Place skewers on grill rack over fire or under the broiler and cook until they turn bright pink, about 2 1/2 – 3 minutes per side. Turn with long-handled tongs.

Serve immediately; carefully slide off skewers and squeeze lemon over shrimp.

Makes 8

Stuffed Shrimp

1 1/2 pounds large shrimp (16 count)
1 (2-ounce) tin anchovies (optional)
24 slices bacon, as needed
Garlic pepper
4 tablespoons butter
Garlic powder
Herb seasoning of your choice (herbes de Provence suggested)
Round toothpicks

Cook bacon until opaque and somewhat firm yet bendable. Clean and peel shrimp, leaving tail on if desired, and slice down the back. Place a small sliver of anchovy in slit and wrap bacon around shrimp. Secure opening with a round toothpick.

Heat butter, garlic pepper, garlic powder and herb seasoning in pan; do not let it burn. Grill one side of shrimp until bacon turns slightly brown. Baste top side with butter mixture; turn and grill second side until bacon is browned.

Adjust seasoning to taste.

Makes approximately 16

Cilantro Lime Shrimp

3 large garlic cloves
1 1/8 teaspoons salt
1/2 cup lime juice
1/4 cup sweet orange marmalade
1/4 cup finely chopped cilantro
4 tablespoons olive oil
1 tablespoon soy sauce
1/2 teaspoon red pepper flakes
1/2 teaspoon freshly ground black pepper
1-2 Thai bird chiles, minced (optional)
1 pound large shrimp (21-25 count) peeled and deveined, leaving tail and last section attached

Mince and mash garlic to paste with salt. Whisk together paste, lime juice, marmalade, cilantro, 3 tablespoons oil, soy sauce, pepper flakes and black pepper. Save 1/3 cup of mixture to serve for dipping sauce; chiles can be added to this if using. Combine shrimp with remaining mixture in a large sealable plastic bag, Press out air. Marinate shrimp in refrigerator, turning bag once, 15 minutes.

Drain shrimp and pat dry. Heat 1 1/2 teaspoons oil in a 12-inch nonstick skillet over moderately high heat. Add half of the shrimp and cook, turning occasionally, until golden brown and just cooked through, about 3 minutes. Cook remaining shrimp in remaining 1 1/2 teaspoons oil in same manner.

Garnish shrimp with cilantro, if desired, and serve with dipping sauce.

Makes approximately 24 pieces

Shrimp Cheesecake

Takes some time, but oh! so good.

Crust

4 ounces grated Parmesan cheese
1 cup panko (Japanese bread crumbs)
1/2 cup French bread crumbs
1/2 cup pecans, additional for garnish
1/2 teaspoon Creole seasoning
1/2 cups butter, melted

Filling

1 tablespoon olive oil
1 cup chopped onion
1/4 cup chopped celery
1/4 cup chopped green bell pepper
1/2 cup chopped roasted red pepper
1/4 cup chopped green onions
1 (16-ounce) package cream cheese
12 ounces smoked Gouda cheese, grated
8 ounces goat cheese
4 ounces fresh Parmesan cheese, grated
1/2 cup heavy cream
4 eggs, beaten
1 pound shrimp, cooked, roughly chopped
1/4 pound Andouille sausage, finely diced

Crust: Preheat oven to 325 degrees. Combine cheese, crumbs, pecans and seasoning in food processor and pulse until mixture is finely ground. Remove mixture and work butter in until combined. Press into bottom of springform pan (10-inch or 9 x 12-inch) and bake 15 minutes or until brown.

Filling: In a baking pan large enough to accommodate the springform pan, add an inch or so of water to make a water bath. Cut and place a piece of foil large enough to encircle springform pan so no water can leak into it.

Sauté vegetables in olive oil until tender, set aside to cool. Beat cheeses in mixer until smooth; add heavy cream and eggs and mix.

Gently fold seafood, sausage and vegetables into cheese mixture. Pour into crust, place in water bath and bake 1 1/2 hours or until set.

Serves 16 to 20

Candlelight Smoked Salmon Cheesecake

Use for an elegant dinner party

3 (3-inch) slices French bread
1 teaspoon butter, melted (more if needed)
4 (8-ounce) packages cream cheese, softened
1 cup sour cream
1/2 cup whipping cream
3 eggs
1 1/2 teaspoons fresh lime juice
1 1/2 teaspoons chopped fresh dill
1/2 pound smoked salmon, skinless, sliced very thin

Topping

1 (8-ounce) package cream cheese
1/2 cup sour cream

Preheat oven to 350 degrees. Chop bread in a food processor until fine, add melted butter and process 5 seconds. Place crumb mixture in bottom of 9-inch springform pan. Spread evenly over bottom with fork; do not make it too thick. Bake until crumbs are golden brown. Cool.

Place softened cream cheese in mixer and mix until smooth. Using low speed, add sour cream a little at a time and mix in cream until smooth. Add eggs, one at a time and mix well.

Place a layer of cheese filling to cover bottom of pan; next a layer of salmon. Repeat layers until pan is full, ending with cheese mixture. Bake at 300 degrees 2 hours. Turn off heat and let cake remain in oven 1 hour longer. Chill overnight.

When ready to serve, blend topping and spread over cake. Place in center of 250 degree oven 10 minutes. Cool before serving.

Thai Chicken Meatballs

Ted Habiger, Room 39
1719 West 38th Street, Kansas City, MO

2 pounds boneless chicken thigh meat, ground
2 lemons, juiced
1/4 cup ginger, minced
8 scallions, thinly sliced green part only
1/2 cup sweet chili sauce (Mai Ploy)*
2 tablespoons coriander seeds, toasted and ground
1/4 cup cilantro, minced
3/4 cup panko (Japanese bread crumbs) plus more for coating

Mix all above ingredients together. Form into small balls no larger than a quarter. Roll in panko to coat. Deep fry at 325 degrees. Serve with a side of sweet chili sauce.

Makes 10 to 20

*Mai Ploy or Sweet Chili Sauce is available at most Asian markets, especially those with Thai food.

Teriyaki Beef Nuggets

1/3 cup soy sauce
2 tablespoons honey
1/2 teaspoon ground ginger
1-2 cloves garlic, crushed
1 teaspoon grated onion
1/4 cup dry white wine
3/4-1 pound top sirloin, cut into 1/2-inch diagonal slices
1 (5-ounce) can water chestnuts
Wooden picks

In a shallow bowl combine soy sauce, honey, ginger, garlic, onion and wine. Wrap one slice of meat around each water chestnut half and secure with wooden pick. Marinate beef nuggets in soy mixture for one hour. Place nuggets on broiler pan and broil 3-4 minutes on rack 5-8 inches from heat, turning once or twice.

Makes approximately 24 pieces

Note: Serve nuggets with Tamarind Date Sweet & Sour Sauce. Can be found at India Emporium or other Indian grocery stores.

Hanky Pankies (Polish Mistakes)

1 pound ground beef
1 pound spicy sausage
1 pound Velveeta cheese
1 teaspoon garlic powder
1 teaspoon oregano
2 loaves Pepperidge Farm Party Rye

Preheat oven to 350 degrees. Brown and drain meat, melt cheese and mix together, add seasonings and mix well. Spoon mixture onto pieces of rye, approximately 2 teaspoons on each.

Bake uncovered 15 minutes.

Note: It is suggested to double the recipe and freeze half.

Baked Little Smokies

1 (14-ounce) package little smokies
1 (8-ounce) package crescent rolls

Sauce

1/4 cup butter, melted
1/2 cup chopped pecans, optional
3 tablespoons honey
3 tablespoons brown sugar

Preheat oven to 400 degrees. Press seams of roll dough together to form 1 large piece. Cut dough into strips. Roll smokies in strips of dough and place in 8 x 8-inch pan.

Sauce: Mix together all sauce ingredients and pour over the top of rolls. Bake for 20 minutes.

Water Chestnuts with Bacon & Sauce

Remember this? It is still good.

2 (8-ounce) cans water chestnuts
1 pound bacon

Sauce

1 cup sugar
1/2 cup water
1/2 cup vinegar
1 tablespoon freshly ground pepper
1 1/2 teaspoons salt
2 tablespoons cornstarch
1 tablespoon water

Wrap bacon pieces to fit around each chestnut. Secure with toothpick. Place on broiler pan and cook until bacon is done, turning once.

Sauce: Combine sugar, water, vinegar, salt and pepper. Add cornstarch mixed with water to thicken sauce if necessary.

Pizza Dip

Crust

1 (8-ounce) package cream cheese
1/2 cup sour cream
1/2 teaspoon garlic salt
1/4 cup Parmesan cheese

Filling

1 (7-8-ounce) jar pizza sauce
1 cup mozzarella cheese
Tomato, drained and chopped
Mushrooms, chopped
Black olives, sliced
Green pepper, chopped
Red onion, chopped
Parmesan cheese

Crust

Mix ingredients and spread in a round pie plate.

Filling

Preheat oven to 350 degrees. Spread pizza sauce on crust and cover with mozzarella cheese. Place vegetables of your choice on top and add a few shakes of Parmesan. Bake for 20-25 minutes.

Serve with crackers, lavosh, etc.

Pepperoni Pizza Dip

1 (8-ounce) package cream cheese
1/2 cup sour cream
1 teaspoon dried oregano
1/2 teaspoon garlic powder
1/4 teaspoon crushed red pepper, optional
1/2 cup pizza sauce
1/2 cup chopped pepperoni
1/4 cup sliced green onion
1/4 cup chopped green pepper
1/2 cup shredded mozzarella cheese

Preheat oven to 350 degrees. Mix together cream cheese, sour cream, oregano, garlic and red pepper. Spread evenly in a 9 or 10-inch quiche dish or pie plate and cover with pizza sauce. Sprinkle pepperoni, onion and pepper over top. Bake 10 minutes, top with cheese and bake 5 minutes longer. Serve with sturdy crackers, corn or tortilla chips.

Wonton Appetizers

1 (16-ounce) package wonton wrappers
Olive oil
1 1/2 cups shredded Cheddar cheese
1 1/2 cups shredded Monterey Jack cheese
1 pound hot sausage, cooked and drained
1 red pepper, diced (optional)
1 (1-ounce) package dry ranch dressing mix, prepared (use 1 cup in recipe)

Preheat oven to 350 degrees. Separate wonton wrappers and lightly brush both sides with olive oil. Place in mini muffin cup tins and bake 5-7 minutes until light brown on edges.

Combine rest of ingredients and fill cups. Bake again until filling is melted and bubbly, 5-7 minutes. Serve warm.

Hot Pecan Dip

- 1 (8-ounce) package cream cheese, softened
- 2 tablespoons whole milk
- 1 (3-4-ounce) package dried beef
- 1/4 cup green pepper
- 1/2 teaspoon garlic salt
- 1/2 cup sour cream
- 1/2 cup chopped pecans
- 2 tablespoons butter

Preheat oven to 350 degrees Blend cream cheese with milk. Chop or tear dried beef and add to mixture along with pepper and garlic salt. Mix in sour cream and spoon mixture into an 8-inch pie pan or similar serving dish.

Melt butter and brown pecans. Toss with salt and sprinkle over cheese. Bake for 20 minutes or until hot and bubbly. Serve with crackers or small cocktail bread.

Spinach Artichoke Dip

This is tried and true.

- 1 (14-ounce) can artichoke hearts, quartered
- 1/2 (10-ounce) box frozen spinach, thawed
- 1 cup mayonnaise
- 1 cup shredded Parmesan cheese
- 1/2 teaspoon garlic salt
- 1/4 teaspoon red pepper flakes
- Cayenne pepper

Preheat oven to 375 degrees. Combine all ingredients except cayenne pepper, place in shallow baking dish and sprinkle lightly with cayenne. Bake 20 minutes, until bubbly. Serve with crackers or tortilla chips.

Note: This can be easily doubled.

Artichoke and Parmesan Spread

Quick and Easy

- 2 (14-ounce) cans artichoke hearts, wedged
- 3 tablespoons extra virgin olive oil
- 1/2 cup chopped flat leaf parsley
- 1 cup grated Parmesan cheese
- 1/4 teaspoon kosher salt
- 1/4 teaspoon pepper

Combine all ingredients, serve with large crackers.

Artichoke & Roasted Red Pepper Dip

2 tablespoons butter
1 leek, diced
1 (13-ounce) jar marinated artichoke hearts, drained and chopped
1 (7-ounce) jar roasted red pepper, drained and chopped
3/4 cup freshly grated Parmesan cheese
3 tablespoons mayonnaise
3 tablespoons milk

Preheat oven to 350 degrees. Melt butter in sauce pan over medium heat and sauté leek until tender. Stir in artichokes, peppers, cheese, mayonnaise and milk. Transfer to an 8 x 8-inch baking dish. Bake 30 minutes or until bubbly and lightly browned.

Pesto Tart

1 (32-ounce) carton plain yogurt, drained for 24 hours
1 cup dry bread crumbs
2 tablespoons olive oil
2 large eggs
1/2 cup pesto
1 cup grated Parmesan
Salt and pepper to taste

Preheat oven to 350 degrees. Combine yogurt and crumbs for crust and press into bottom and up sides of an 8-inch springform pan. Bake crust 5-7 minutes until lightly browned. Whisk together remaining ingredients and pour over crust. Bake 45 minutes until set.

Serve with a light cracker.

Sweet Basil Pesto

Cal-Ann Farms, producers of Living Basil Plants found in most area grocery stores.

2 cups Living Basil leaves
2 garlic cloves, peeled and chopped
1 cup walnuts
1 cup extra virgin olive oil
1 cup grated Parmesan
1/4 cup grated Romano
Salt and pepper to taste

Combine basil, garlic and walnuts in food processor; add olive oil in slow steady stream. Add cheeses, salt and pepper. This will keep for 2 weeks or more in refrigerator.

Note: Use in soups or spread on toast points as an appetizer. Makes enough for two pounds of pasta.

Onion Tartlets

4 tablespoons unsalted butter
2 1/2 cups Vidalia onion, chopped
1 1/2 teaspoons fine herbs or Herbes de Provence
1 (15-ounce) box refrigerated pie crust
1/2 cup half-and-half
1 large egg, lightly beaten
1/2 of (1-ounce) package onion soup mix
1/2 cup shredded Parmesan cheese

Preheat oven to 350 degrees. Spray 3 mini muffin pans (36 cups) with Pam.

Melt butter in a large nonstick pan over medium heat and cook onions 17-18 minutes until golden, stirring occasionally. Remove from heat and stir in dried herbs. Allow to cool.

Unroll one sheet of pie dough and use a 2 1/2-inch round cutter to cut out 12 -13 rounds. Reserve scraps and repeat with second sheet of dough. Roll out scraps and continue cutting to make a total of 36 rounds. Gently press each round into cups and bake 11 minutes.

Whisk together half-and-half, egg and onion soup mix, set aside.

Place a heaping 1/2 teaspoon onion in each pastry shell. Slowly pour egg mixture into shell; do not overfill. Sprinkle each top with a scant 1/2 teaspoon Parmesan.

Bake about 25-30 minutes or until golden. Serve warm.

Makes 36

Vidalia Onion Appetizer

1 cup rough chopped Vidalia or other sweet onion, packed
1 cup grated Swiss cheese, packed (imported if available)
1 cup mayonnaise, regular or light
1 tablespoon fresh lemon juice

Preheat oven to 400 degrees. Mix onion, cheese and mayonnaise; stir in lemon juice. Bake 20 minutes, or until lightly browned.

Serve with baguette slices or crackers.

Note: Recipe can be increased; use equal proportions of cheese, onions and mayonnaise but always use 1 tablespoon of lemon juice.

Portobello Brie Cups

6 ounces Portobello mushroom, finely chopped
2 tablespoons butter
1 teaspoon Dijon mustard
1 (8-ounce) can refrigerated crescent rolls
3 ounces Brie cheese

Preheat oven to 375 degrees. Spray 24 mini muffin cups. In a small skillet combine mushrooms, butter and garlic. Cook over medium heat 5-6 minutes or until butter is absorbed and mushrooms are tender, stirring occasionally. Stir in mustard.

Separate dough into four rectangles and seal perforations. Cut each rectangle into 6 squares. Press one square of dough into each muffin cup, letting corners stand above top of cups. Spoon about one tablespoon mushroom mixture into each.

Bake10-12 minutes until light golden brown. While baking, cut Brie into 24 pieces. Remove cups from oven and place a piece of Brie on muffin tops. Return to oven and bake an additional 2-4 minutes until cheese is softened. Cool slightly before serving.

Makes 24

Mushroom Pâté

4 tablespoons butter, divided
8 ounces fresh mushrooms, minced
1 1/2 teaspoons minced garlic
1/4 cup minced green onion, white only
1/3 cup chicken stock
1/2 (8-ounce) package cream cheese, softened
2 tablespoons minced green onions, green only
2 teaspoons Worcestershire sauce
2 teaspoons fresh lemon juice
1 1/2 teaspoons minced fresh thyme
1 teaspoon salt, optional
Freshly ground black pepper
Parsley, chopped
Red bell pepper, chopped
Green onion, chopped

Melt 2 tablespoons butter in medium skillet, add mushrooms and sauté 2-3 minutes. Add garlic and green onion and sauté 1 minute. Add chicken stock and cook over high heat until all liquid is absorbed. Cool to room temperature.

Blend cream cheese and remaining 2 tablespoons butter, add mushroom mixture, green onions, Worcestershire, lemon juice, thyme, salt and pepper. Adjust seasonings. Pour into 1-cup mold, lined with plastic wrap, and chill.

When ready to serve, unmold onto serving plate and sprinkle with parsley, red pepper or green onions. Serve with toast points or crackers.

Note: This can be prepared up to 3 days in advance.

Blue Cheese Puffs

2 (8-ounce) packages cream cheese
1 cup mayonnaise
1 tablespoon fresh minced onion
1/4 cup minced chives
1 cup blue cheese crumbles
1/4-1/2 tablespoon cayenne pepper
1 (16-ounce loaf) Pepperidge Farm Very Thin sliced bread
Paprika

Mix all ingredients except bread and paprika. Spread mixture on bread slices, approximately 1/4 cup per slice. Cut diagonally into triangles. Place on cookie sheet and freeze.

For serving, preheat oven to 350 degrees, remove from freezer and bake 15 minutes. Sprinkle with paprika and serve warm.

Makes 50 to 60

Easily halved for smaller groups.

Sun-Dried Tomato Spread

1/2 cup oil packed sun-dried tomatoes (use oil)
1/4 cup chopped fresh dill
1 (8-ounce) package cream cheese, softened
1/2 cup butter, softened
1 clove garlic, crushed
1/2 cup shredded Parmesan cheese
Salt and pepper to taste

Place all ingredients in food processor; pulse and chill.

Serve with bagel chips.

Cranberry-Blue Cheese Ball

Pretty at holiday time.

4 ounces sharp white Cheddar cheese, grated
1 (8-ounce) package cream cheese
4 ounces crumbled blue cheese
1 (6-ounce) bag sweetened dried cranberries

Combine all ingredients. Scoop onto a sheet of plastic wrap and form into a ball. Refrigerate overnight. Bring to room temperature before serving.

Serve with graham cracker sticks, ginger snaps or Carr Wheat Crackers.

Raspberry Chipotle Cheese Ring

1 pound Cheddar cheese, shredded
3/4 cup mayonnaise
1 medium onion, finely chopped
1 clove garlic, pressed
1/2 teaspoon Tabasco sauce
1 cup chopped pecans
1 (15-ounce) Bronco Bob's Raspberry Chipotle Sauce

Mix all ingredients except sauce and place in a round mold or Bundt pan (something with an open center). Line container with plastic wrap to help unmold. Chill. Pour sauce into bowl that will fit into the center of the ring. Arrange crackers around ring. Put a bit of cheese on cracker and top with sauce.

Feta Cheese Appetizers

1/2 cup finely chopped onion
3 cloves garlic, minced
2 teaspoons olive oil
1 teaspoon sesame oil
1 (8-ounce) package cream cheese, cut up
4 ounces crumbled feta cheese
1/2 cup pitted kalamata olives or ripe olives
1/4 cup chopped roasted red sweet peppers
1 teaspoon dried dill
3 pita bread rounds

Preheat broiler. In a medium skillet cook onion and garlic in oils over medium heat 4-5 minutes or until onion is tender. Remove from heat and add cheeses; stir until mixture is nearly smooth. Stir in olives, peppers and dill. Set aside

Split pita rounds in half horizontally to form two circles. Place, cut side up, on a large plain baking sheet. Broil 3 inches from heat 1 minute or until lightly toasted.

Spread each round with about 1/3 cup of cheese mixture. Broil about 1 minute more or until hot. Cut each round into six wedges with a sharp knife or scissors before serving.

Makes 36

Feta and Walnut Spread

1 cup walnut halves, toasted
1 1/2 cups feta cheese crumbles
1/2 cup milk
1 teaspoon dried oregano
1/4 cup flat-leaf parsley, chopped
Freshly ground black pepper
1/2 teaspoon crushed red pepper flakes

Place all ingredients in food processor and mix until of a spreadable consistency. Serve with pita chips.

Note: Cut pita pockets into triangles, drizzle them with olive oil, parsley and oregano and bake till brown and crispy. Watch closely; this does not take long.

Tomato Basil Cheese Spread

1 cup low-fat ricotta cheese
3 ounces fresh goat cheese
1/2 cup sun-dried tomatoes, (not packed in oil)
2 cloves garlic, minced
2-3 Roma tomatoes, seeded and diced
1/4 cup chopped fresh basil
1 tablespoon extra virgin olive oil
1/4 teaspoon salt
1/4 teaspoon freshly ground pepper
1 tablespoon pine nuts, toasted
Basil leaves for garnish (optional)

With a mixer combine cheeses until smooth. Spread mixture evenly in bottom of a shallow dish; cover and refrigerate. Cut sun-dried tomatoes into small pieces and cover with boiling water. Allow sun-dried tomatoes to soak for 20-30 minutes, drain.

Combine tomatoes, garlic, basil, olive oil, salt and pepper. Blend well and spoon over cheese. Sprinkle with pine nuts. Garnish with basil leaves, if desired, and serve with crackers.

Dried Fruit Ball

1 (16-ounce) package cream cheese, softened
1 (7-ounce) package Del Monte or Sun Maid Fruit Bits
4 tablespoons frozen orange juice concentrate
1/2 cup chopped nuts

Mix cream cheese, orange juice and fruit. Chill overnight. (This may look as if it won't work but do not fear, it will). Roll in nuts and serve with gingersnaps.

Note: A great brunch appetizer.

BLT Dip

It really tastes like a BLT sandwich!

1 pound bacon fried crisp (crumbled in blender)
1 cup mayonnaise
1 cup sour cream
2 tomatoes, seeded, diced

Fold all ingredients together and serve with bagel chips or cracker of your choice.

Mexicorn Dip

2 (11-ounce) cans Mexicorn, drained
1 cup sour cream
1 cup mayonnaise
3 green onions, chopped
1 (4-ounce) can chopped green chilies
1/4-1/2 (16-ounce) jar jalapeno peppers, chopped or to taste
1 cup shredded Cheddar cheese

Combine all ingredients and chill before serving. Serve with tortilla chips.

Bean Dip

1 (15-ounce) can white beans
2-3 tablespoons olive oil
1 small bunch fresh chives, finely chopped
1 garlic clove, minced
1/2 teaspoon kosher salt
1 1/2 teaspoons lemon juice
1 teaspoon chopped fresh parsley
Bruschetta
Freshly grated Parmesan

Rinse beans and place in food processor. While processing, slowly add oil until dip is smooth and creamy. Add remaining ingredients and pulse to combine.

Spread on bruschetta and top with Parmesan. If using as a dip, place in bowl with Parmesan on top and serve with fresh vegetables.

Note: Oregano, dill or other herbs may be added to alter the flavor.

Black-Eyed Pea Salsa

- 1 cup frozen yellow corn
- 1 (15-ounce) can black-eyed peas
- 2 cloves garlic
- 1/2 cup cilantro leaves, loosely packed, stems removed
- 1 (14-ounce) can Mexican-style stewed tomatoes
- 1/2 cup thinly sliced green onions
- Juice of 1/2 lime
- Tortilla chips

Place corn and peas in a colander. Rinse both well with cool water until corn begins to defrost. Drain well, shaking colander to remove excess water. Place corn and peas in a 2- quart bowl.

In blender or food processor finely chop garlic; add cilantro and pulse to chop fine. Squeeze in lime juice. Add tomatoes and pulse 2-3 times but do not over process. Pour mixture over peas and corn. Add onions and stir well to mix. Transfer to serving bowl and serve with chips.

Marinated Olives

- 2 (12-ounce) canning jars or 4 (8-ounce), well cleaned
- 1 (21-ounce dry weight) jar queen size green olives, drained, retain juice
- 4 teaspoons coriander seeds crushed
- 2 teaspoons dried thyme
- 2 teaspoons dried rosemary crushed
- 6-8 garlic cloves, thinly sliced
- 1-2 anchovies, optional
- 2-4 bay leaves
- 4 tablespoons sherry vinegar
- Fresh rosemary, optional

Drain olives, keeping juice in reserve. Divide all herbs into jars with sliced garlic and anchovies, if using. Return olives to jars. Fill with vinegar and juice. Place lids and shake well. Refrigerate for several days before use. Shake every few days. Will keep 4-6 months.

Note: Good for a gift. Garnish with rosemary, in or tied to the jar.

Buttered Roasted Almonds or Pecans

3 tablespoons butter
1 pound whole raw almonds or pecans
1 1/2 tablespoons kosher salt

Turn slow cooker to high and melt butter. Once melted, turn cooker to low. Add nuts and stir to coat with butter. Cover and cook on low 2 hours, stirring several times during cooking. When done, add salt and toss well to coat. Let nuts cool, uncovered, and store in a tightly sealed container.

Herbes de Provence Nuts

1 cup walnuts
1 cup almonds
1 1/2 teaspoons extra virgin olive oil
1 1/4 teaspoons herbes de Provence
1/4 teaspoon salt
1/4 teaspoon sugar

Toast nuts, 1 cup at a time, in microwave 4 minutes at medium power. Drizzle with olive oil and sprinkle with herbes de Provence, salt and sugar; adjust to taste. Serve warm or at room temperature.

Cheddar Crisps

1 3/4 cups flour
1/2 cup yellow cornmeal
1/2 teaspoon sugar
1/2 teaspoon baking soda
1/2 teaspoon salt
1/2 cup butter
1 1/2 cups shredded extra sharp Cheddar cheese
2 tablespoons white vinegar
Coarsely ground black pepper

Mix flour, cornmeal, baking soda, sugar and salt. Cut in butter until mixture resembles coarse crumbs (may use food processor). Stir in cheese, vinegar and 1/2 cup cold water until mixture forms a soft dough. Shape dough into a ball, wrap in plastic and refrigerate 1 hour or until dough is firm.

Preheat oven to 375 degrees. Grease large cookie sheet. On a lightly floured surface, with floured rolling pin, roll 1/4 of dough into a paper thin round about 13 inches in diameter; edges may be ragged. (Keep remaining dough refrigerated). Cut dough into 8 wedges. Sprinkle with coarsely ground pepper and press into dough. Place on sheet and bake about 10 minutes or until browned and crisp. Cool on racks. Repeat with remaining dough. Store in tightly covered container.

Makes 32

Breakfasts, Brunches & Breads

Farm to Market Bread Co.

Menu Ideas

Breakfasts, Brunches & Breads

Breakfast Risotto

- 4 hot Italian sausages, casings removed
- 2 tablespoons butter
- 1 small onion, diced
- 1 cup Arborio rice
- 1/2 cup dry white wine
- 2 small bay leaves
- 3 cups low sodium chicken broth (more may be needed)
- Pinch of saffron threads
- 1/3 cup freshly grated Parmesan cheese (additional for garnish)
- 1/3 cup chopped Italian parsley (additional for garnish)
- Salt and pepper to taste

Brown sausage in skillet, drain excess grease, set aside. In a separate heavy bottomed saucepan melt butter and sauté onion until translucent, about 4 minutes; stir in rice. Add wine; stir until liquid evaporates, about 1 minute.

Add broth, saffron and bay leaves; bring to boil. Reduce heat to medium-low; add cooked sausage, simmer, stirring occasionally, until risotto is tender, adding more broth if dry, about 18 minutes.

Discard bay leaves; mix in Parmesan and parsley. Season with salt and pepper; garnish as desired.

Serves 4

Spicy Bacon with Cayenne Pepper

- 1 1/2 tablespoons light brown sugar, packed
- 1/4-1/2 teaspoon cayenne pepper
- 1/4 teaspoon black pepper
- 1 pound thick-cut bacon, about 12 slices

Preheat oven to 350 degrees and place rack in middle of oven. Stir together brown sugar, cayenne and black pepper in a small bowl.

Arrange bacon slices in 1 layer, not overlapping, on rack of a large broiler pan. Bake 20 minutes; turn slices and sprinkle evenly with spiced sugar. Continue baking until crisp and deep golden, 20 to 35 minutes more, checking bacon every 5 minutes. Transfer to paper towels to drain.

Note: These are great for BLT sandwiches with avocado.

Parmesan Grits

- 1 cup uncooked regular grits
- 1 1/4 cups milk
- 1 (14-ounce) can chicken broth
- 1 (10 3/4-ounce) can cream of celery soup
- 1 cup grated Parmesan cheese
- 3 tablespoons butter
- 2 tablespoons chopped fresh basil
- 2 tablespoons grated Parmesan cheese

Preheat oven to 350 degrees. Bring grits, milk and broth to a boil in a medium saucepan over medium-high heat; reduce heat to low and simmer, stirring occasionally, 4-5 minutes or until thickened. Remove from heat; stir in soup and next 3 ingredients. Pour mixture into a lightly greased 8-inch square baking dish.

Bake 30 minutes. Top evenly with grated Parmesan.

Serves 6

Note: Feature grits the next time you entertain. Serve several toppings such as the ones listed below so guests can mix in their favorite flavors:

Gravy
Pesto
Shredded cheeses
Roasted vegetables
Crumbled bacon
Grilled corn kernels
Salsas
Cilantro

Jalapeno and Fresh Horseradish Bloody Marys

- 2 quarts tomato juice
- 1 cup vodka
- Juice of 3 lemons
- 4 jalapenos, cored, seeded and minced
- 1/4 cup horseradish root, grated
- 1 tablespoon Worcestershire sauce
- Freshly ground black pepper
- Celery salt
- Ice
- Celery sticks

Combine tomato juice, vodka, lemon juice, jalapenos, horseradish and Worcestershire sauce in a pitcher. Stir well; season to taste with pepper and celery salt. Fill 6 glasses with ice and divide mixture among glasses; garnish with celery sticks.

Sweet Potato Hash with Bacon

1/2 pound bacon, cut into 1/4-inch strips
2 medium onions, chopped
1 large red bell pepper, cut into thin strips
2 pounds sweet potatoes, peeled, cut into 1/2-inch cubes
1 teaspoon chopped fresh thyme
Salt and pepper

Cook bacon over medium heat until crisp. Transfer to paper towels and reserve fat in skillet. Add onions, bell pepper, salt and pepper and cook, stirring occasionally, until vegetables are softened. Stir in potatoes and cook, covered, stirring occasionally, until potatoes are tender and starting to brown, 10 to 14 minutes. Stir in thyme and bacon and adjust seasonings.

Serves 6

Dill Smoked Salmon Hash

4 tablespoons butter
3 cups frozen southern-style hash brown potatoes (cubed)
1 cup chopped onion
1/4 cup whipping cream
1/4 pound smoked peppered salmon, diced
2 teaspoons chopped fresh dill
Salt and pepper

Melt butter in large nonstick skillet over medium-low heat. Add potatoes and onion. Cover skillet and cook until potatoes and onion are softened and beginning to brown, about 10 minutes. Add cream and increase heat to medium and cook until most of cream is absorbed and mixture is moist, stirring often, about 2 minutes. Mix in salmon and dill. Season with salt and pepper.

Serves 4 to 6

Best Ever Sticky Buns

Adapted from Beautiful Breakfasts and Brunches

Dough

2 cups water
2 medium potatoes, peeled and cubed
1/3 cup sugar
6 tablespoons butter, softened and cubed
1 teaspoon salt
1 egg, room temperature
1 egg yolk
1 envelope dry yeast
4 1/2 cups bread flour, plus additional for kneading and rolling

Filling

4 tablespoons butter
1/3 cup sugar
2 teaspoons cinnamon

Glaze

1/2 pound butter plus 4 tablespoons, melted
2 cups light brown sugar, packed
1/3 cup dark corn syrup
1 cup chopped walnuts (4 ounces)

For dough, bring water to a boil in a medium saucepan. Add potatoes and cook, covered, until tender. Drain and reserve 1 cup water. Mash potatoes and measure 2/3 cup; save remainder for another use. In large bowl with an electric mixer, mix together potatoes, sugar, butter, salt, potato water, egg, egg yolk and yeast. Add flour and mix on low speed until incorporated. Mix on medium speed 1 minute; dough will be sticky.

Knead with a dough hook 4 to 5 minutes or turn onto well-floured board and knead until smooth and elastic, 8 to 10 minutes. Transfer to a large oiled bowl, turn to grease all sides and cover loosely with greased plastic wrap and a damp towel. Let rise in a warm place until doubled in bulk, about 1 1/2 hours. Punch dough down and let rest for 10 minutes.

While dough rests, make filling by melting butter in a small bowl; stir sugar and cinnamon together.

For glaze mix melted butter, brown sugar and corn syrup. Generously butter two 8-inch or 9-inch round cake pans. Pour half the glaze into bottom of each pan; sprinkle each with 1/2 cup nuts.

On heavily floured surface roll half the dough into a 10 x 16-inch rectangle, about 1/4 inch thick. Brush with 2 tablespoons melted butter. Sprinkle with half the cinnamon sugar. Starting at short end, roll up dough as for a jelly roll. Repeat with second half. Cut each roll into 10 (3/4-inch) slices. Arrange 10 slices in each

(Continued on next page)

Best Ever Sticky Buns *(continued)*
prepared pan. Cover with greased plastic wrap and damp towel and let rise in a warm place until doubled in bulk, about 1 hour.

Preheat oven to 350 degrees. Bake in center of oven 25 to 30 minutes or until golden brown, rotating pans half way through baking time. Remove from oven and let rest 5 minutes for glaze to set; invert onto serving platters. If nuts stick to bottom of pan, loosen with spatula and spread over top.

Makes 20 buns.

Note: Buns may be wrapped in foil and kept at room temperature overnight or frozen.

Sugar and Spice Bacon

1/2 cup all-purpose flour
1/2 cup brown sugar
1 teaspoon black pepper, coarsely ground
1 pound thick cut bacon

Preheat oven to 400 degrees. Combine flour, sugar and pepper in a plastic bag and shake to mix. Shake a few bacon strips at a time with flour mixture to coat. Place coated bacon onto a baking sheet or broiler pan.

Bake 15 minutes or until bacon has cooked.

Note: Great for BLT sandwiches.

Sour Cream Coffee Cake

1/2 pound butter
2 cups sugar
2 cups flour
2 eggs
1 teaspoon baking powder
1/2 teaspoon salt
1 cup sour cream
1 teaspoon vanilla
3/4 cup chopped walnuts or pecans
1 teaspoon cinnamon, heaping
2 tablespoons brown sugar, heaping

Preheat oven to 350 degrees. Cream butter and sugar. Add eggs one at a time, beating 2 minutes after each. Add flour, baking powder and salt. Mix in sour cream and vanilla; batter will be stiff. Spoon half batter mixture into greased and floured bundt pan. Combine nuts, cinnamon and brown sugar and sprinkle over batter. Add remaining batter.

Bake 1 hour. Let cool in pan 15 minutes before removing.

Dust top of cake with powdered sugar.

Strawberry Rhubarb Coffee Cake

2 1/4 cups flour
3/4 cup butter
3/4 cup sugar
1 teaspoon baking powder
1/2 teaspoon baking soda
3/4 teaspoon cinnamon
1/8 teaspoon salt
1 egg, beaten
1 1/2 teaspoons vanilla
3/4 cup buttermilk
Vegetable cooking spray
1 1/2 cups Strawberry/Rhubarb Puree, recipe below
Powdered sugar, optional

Combine flour and sugar; cut in butter with fork or pastry blender until mixture is crumbly. Set aside 1/2 cup of mixture. Add baking powder, baking soda, cinnamon and salt to remaining mixture. Mix in egg, vanilla and buttermilk to make a soft batter.

Preheat oven to 350 degrees. Coat a 9-inch spring form pan with spray and spread 2/3 of batter along bottom and side of pan. Spread Strawberry/Rhubarb Puree on top. Spoon or dollop remaining batter over puree layer. Pull tip of a knife gently through pan to blend batter and puree. Sprinkle reserved flour/sugar mixture on top. Cover edges with aluminum foil to prevent burning. Bake 45 to 50 minutes or until cake tests done. Dust with powdered sugar if desired.

Serves 8 to 10

Strawberry/Rhubarb Puree

2 cups rhubarb, 1-inch cubes
1 cup sugar
2 cups strawberries, hulled

Combine rhubarb and sugar in a mixing bowl; let sit 15 to 30 minutes until juices form. Add strawberries and cook over medium heat in a saucepan, stirring occasionally, 10 to 15 minutes or until fruit is dissolved and puree is smooth and thickened. Refrigerate until needed. This will hold several days.

Makes 1 1/2 to 2 cups.

Mom's Mini Cini's

2 (8-ounce) cans refrigerated crescent rolls
6 tablespoons butter, softened
1/2 cup brown sugar, firmly packed
1/4 cup chopped pecans
1 tablespoon sugar
1 teaspoon cinnamon

Glaze

2/3 cup powdered sugar
1 tablespoon milk or half-and-half
1/4 teaspoon almond extract
1/8 teaspoon salt

Preheat oven to 375 degrees. Separate dough to form 4 rectangles; press perforations to seal.

Mix butter and next 4 ingredients; spread evenly over 1 side of each rectangle. Roll up jellyroll fashion, starting at long end. With a serrated knife gently cut each log into 6 (1-inch thick) slices. Place rolls 1/4 inch apart in two greased 8-inch cake pans.

Bake 15-18 minutes or until golden brown. Make glaze and drizzle over warm rolls.

Artichoke and Cheese Brunch Dish

10 large eggs
1/2 cup flour
1 teaspoon baking powder
1 (16-ounce) container small curd cottage cheese
2 cups pepper Jack cheese, grated
2 cups sharp Cheddar cheese, grated
4 ounces butter
1 teaspoon seasoning salt
1/4 teaspoon pepper
1 teaspoon basil
1 medium onion
1 (13-ounce) can artichoke hearts, drained and chopped
Salsa

Pre heat oven to 350 degrees. Slightly beat eggs and blend in flour and baking powder. Add cheeses. Sauté onions in butter and add salt, pepper and basil. Add artichokes to onion mixture and combine with rest of ingredients. Bake 45-60 minutes in oiled casserole. Serve with side bowl of salsa.

Serves 10

Sausage in Puff Pastry

1 pound bulk sausage, pork or turkey
1 medium onion, chopped
1 cup shredded Cheddar or Gouda cheese
1 cup apple, peeled and grated
1 (17-ounce) frozen puff pastry, thawed
2 tablespoons milk

Preheat oven to 400 degrees. Brown sausage and onion, breaking up sausage; drain. Combine sausage, cheese and apple, mixing well. Set aside.

Roll out one sheet of pastry on a lightly floured surface to a 10 x 15- inch rectangle. Spread half of sausage mixture lengthwise down the middle of pastry. Cut pastry from edge to filling into 1-inch wide strips. Fold alternating strips over filling in a criss-cross pattern to look like a braid. Repeat with remaining pastry and sausage mixture.

Carefully transfer pastry to a greased baking sheet. Brush top with milk. Bake 25 to 30 minutes or until golden brown.

Serves 12

Note: This freezes well. Thaw completely before cooking.

Carrot-Citrus Booster

Even if you don't care for carrot juice,
you're sure to enjoy this simple smoothie.

3/4 cup carrot juice
3/4 cup lemon sorbet
8 ice cubes

Pulse in blender.

Note: Champagne may be added to this drink for a brunch cocktail or use as sorbet for a palate cleanser. Very refreshing!

Potato Pancakes with Salmon, Caviar and Dill Cream

1/2 cup crème fraîche or sour cream
1 teaspoon chopped dill
1 teaspoon fresh lemon juice
Kosher salt & freshly ground pepper
1 tablespoon snipped chives
1 pound baking potatoes (2 medium), peeled
1 small onion
1 large egg, lightly beaten
2 tablespoons all purpose flour
1/2 teaspoon baking powder
1 teaspoon salt
1/4 teaspoon pepper
1/2 teaspoon vegetable oil
1/2 pound smoked salmon, thinly sliced
2 ounces caviar

Mix crème fraîche with dill and lemon juice, season with salt and pepper and sprinkle with chives. Refrigerate until ready to serve.

In a food processor or grater, coarsely shred potatoes and onion. Place in a clean towel and squeeze dry.

Combine potatoes and onion with egg, flour, baking powder, 1 teaspoon salt and 1/4 teaspoon black pepper.

Using a large non-stick skillet or griddle, heat vegetable oil until shimmering. Drop scoops of potato mixture onto skillet, flatten with back of spoon to make a 3-inch round. Cook over moderately high heat until golden on the bottom, about 4 minutes. Flip pancakes and cook until golden, about 3 minutes longer. Transfer to paper towels to drain. Repeat with remaining potato mixture.

Arrange warm pancakes on a platter topped with smoked salmon, dill cream and caviar.

Makes about 12 pancakes

Note: A delicious variation is to top with a poached egg to make a potato and salmon benedict.

Night-Before French Toast

1 (10-ounce) loaf 18-inch long thin French bread
8 eggs
3 cups milk
1/4 cup sugar
3/4 teaspoon salt
1 tablespoon vanilla
2 tablespoons butter, cut into 18 pieces
1/2 teaspoon ground cinnamon
Syrup

Generously grease a 13 x 9-inch baking dish. Cut bread into 18 (1-inch wide) slices and place in one layer in bottom of pan.

Thoroughly mix eggs, milk, sugar, salt and vanilla; pour over bread in pan. Bread will float on top of liquid. Dot each piece of bread with butter and sprinkle with cinnamon.

Cover and refrigerate overnight or up to 36 hours.

Place dish, uncovered, in cold oven; turn oven to 350 degrees (325 degrees if using glass dish) and bake 45 to 50 minutes, until bread is puffy and light brown.

Remove from oven. Allow to set for 5 minutes.

Bread will rise to top with layer of custard on the bottom, similar to bread pudding. Serve with maple, raspberry, strawberry or coconut syrups.

Serves 8 to 10

Note: An excellent brunch dish, especially for holiday mornings; goes great with fruit cup.

Champagne Pomegranate Cocktail

2 cups crushed ice
2 cups pomegranate juice
1/2 cup ginger ale
1/4 cup brandy
1 (750 ml) bottle of champagne or sparkling wine
Pomegranate seeds (optional)

Combine first 5 ingredients in pitcher. Pour evenly into 8 glasses and garnish with seeds, if desired.

Stuffed Croissant French Toast

1 (8-ounce) package cream cheese, softened
1/4 cup maple syrup
1 tablespoon granulated sugar
1/2 cup chopped fresh strawberries
4 large (about 6-inch) fresh croissants
3 eggs
1 cup half-and-half or light cream
1 tablespoon brown sugar, packed
1/2 teaspoon cinnamon
1/2 teaspoon nutmeg
Fresh strawberries, halved
Maple syrup

With an electric mixer beat cream cheese, maple syrup and sugar until well combined; stir in strawberries. With serrated knife cut each croissant in half horizontally, cutting to but not through other side. Spoon filling into each croissant.

Whisk together eggs, half and half, brown sugar, cinnamon and nutmeg. Dip each side of croissant in egg mixture, being careful not to squeeze out filling.

Cook filled croissants, two at a time, on lightly greased griddle over medium heat about 1 to 2 minutes on each side. Use two spatulas to turn. Some filling may leak out onto griddle; wipe off griddle and lightly grease before cooking remaining croissants. Serve warm, sprinkled with strawberries and drizzled with syrup.

Serves 4

Champagne and Strawberry Cocktail

2 cups small slices of strawberries
3/4 cup sugar
3 cups dry white wine, such as Sauvignon Blanc or Pinot Grigio
Champagne

Mix 3/4 cups sugar with strawberries. Pour white wine over, mix; cover and refrigerate overnight.

Place 3 tablespoons strawberry mixture into a wine glass and fill with champagne.

Note: Use strawberries and blueberries for a festive Fourth of July cocktail!

Blueberry-Stuffed French Toast

- 12 slices good white bread, crusts removed, cut into 1-inch cubes
- 2 (8-ounce) packages cream cheese, cubed
- 1 cup blueberries
- 2 cups milk
- 12 large eggs
- 1/3 cup maple syrup

Arrange half the bread cubes in a buttered 9 x 13-inch glass baking dish. Scatter cheese over bread and sprinkle with berries. Arrange remaining bread cubes over blueberries. Whisk together eggs, syrup and milk; pour evenly over bread mixture and chill overnight. Bake, covered with foil, on middle rack of 350 degree oven 30 minutes. Remove foil and bake 30 minutes more or until puffed and golden.

Sauce

- 1 cup sugar
- 1 cup water
- 2 tablespoons cornstarch
- 1 cup blueberries
- 1 tablespoon unsalted butter, melted

Combine sugar, cornstarch and water; cook over moderate heat, stirring occasionally, 5 minutes or until thickened. Stir in blueberries and simmer mixture, stirring occasionally, 10 minutes or until blueberries have burst. Add butter and stir until melted.

Serves 8 to 10

Tip

To determine whether an egg is fresh, immerse it in a pan of cool salted water. If it sinks, it is fresh; if it rises to the surface, throw it away.

Sunshine Smoothie

- 1 cup low-fat vanilla yogurt
- 1/4 cup low-fat small curd cottage cheese
- 1/2 cup crushed ice
- 1 cup crushed pineapple
- 1/2 cup white grape juice
- 2 tablespoons coconut syrup (optional)

Combine all ingredients in a blender and process on high 2 – 3 minutes, until smooth. Garnish with pineapple wedges and cherries, if desired.

Note: This is low in fat and high in antioxidants!

Ricotta Pancakes with Blueberries

1 1/2 cups all purpose flour
1 teaspoon baking powder
1 1/2 teaspoons kosher salt
3 large eggs, separated
1 3/4 cups plus 2 tablespoons milk
6 ounces ricotta cheese (1/2 cup plus 2 tablespoons)
1/4 cup sugar
1 tablespoon vanilla
Unsalted butter
2 cups fresh or frozen blueberries, thawed
Maple syrup

Whisk together flour, baking powder and salt. Whisk egg yolks with milk, ricotta, sugar and vanilla. Combine wet and dry ingredients and mix until batter is smooth.

With an electric mixer beat egg whites at medium speed until frothy, then beat at high speed until soft peaks form.

Fold egg whites into batter until no streaks remain.

Heat a griddle and lightly butter. For each pancake ladle 1/4 cup batter onto griddle. Cook over moderately low heat until bottoms are golden and just beginning to set. Sprinkle each pancake with a few blueberries, pressing lightly. Flip pancakes and cook until golden on bottom and cooked through, about 1 minute longer.

Serve with maple syrup and bacon.

Serves 6

Tip

Bacon can be cooked in the oven. Preheat oven to 400 degrees. Pour a small amount of water in bottom of broiler pan; spray the top with Pam and place bacon. Bake 15 minutes or until crisp. Cooked bacon can be frozen. Crumble and use in a recipe or on vegetables.

Sweet Potato Pancakes with Honey-Cinnamon Butter

2 large eggs
1 cup buttermilk, more if needed
2 1/2 tablespoons vegetable oil
1 cup pancake mix
1 pinch nutmeg
1 small sweet potato, boiled, peeled and mashed (about 1 1/2 cups)
1/4 cup unsalted butter, room temperature
1/2 teaspoon honey
1/8 teaspoon cinnamon

Pancakes: Whisk together eggs, buttermilk and oil. Stir in pancake mix and nutmeg until just combined. Fold in sweet potato. If batter seems too thick, add enough buttermilk to make it of pourable consistency.

Working in batches, spoon batter onto greased griddle. Cook until surface bubbles, 2-3 minutes. Flip and cook until golden.

Syrup: Combine butter, honey and cinnamon until smooth. Refrigerate until needed.

Serve topped with honey-cinnamon butter and syrup.

Whole Grain Pancakes with Blueberry-Maple Syrup

1 cup plus 2 tablespoons maple syrup
1 cup frozen blueberries, thawed
2 cups whole grain pancake and waffle mix
2 cups buttermilk
6 tablespoons wheat germ
2 teaspoons vanilla
2 teaspoons cinnamon
2 tablespoons butter

Syrup: Boil 1 cup syrup and blueberries in heavy medium saucepan until reduced to generous 1 cup, about 13 minutes. Cool to lukewarm.

Pancakes: Thoroughly combine mix, next 4 ingredients and 2 tablespoons blueberry syrup (batter will be thick).

Melt 1 tablespoon butter on griddle; drop 1/4 cup batter per pancake onto griddle and quickly spread with back of spoon to a 3 or 4-inch round.

Cook until brown and cooked through, about 2 minutes per side. Repeat with remaining butter and batter. Serve with syrup.

Makes 12

Light Crisp Waffles

- 3/4 cup all-purpose flour
- 1/4 cup cornstarch
- 1/2 teaspoon salt
- 1/2 teaspoon baking powder
- 1/4 teaspoon baking soda
- 3/4 cup buttermilk
- 6-8 tablespoons vegetable oil
- 1 large egg, separated
- 1 tablespoon granulated sugar
- 1/2 teaspoon vanilla

Preheat oven to 200 degrees and heat waffle iron. Mix flour, cornstarch, salt, baking powder and baking soda in medium bowl. Measure buttermilk, milk and vegetable oil in a glass measuring cup; mix in egg yolk and set aside.

In another bowl beat egg white almost to soft peaks. Sprinkle in sugar and continue to beat until peaks are firm and glossy. Beat in vanilla. Pour buttermilk mixture into dry ingredients and whisk until just mixed. Drop whipped egg white onto batter in dollops and fold in with rubber spatula until just incorporated.

Pour batter onto hot waffle iron (1/2 to 2/3 cup, depending on size of waffle iron) and cook until waffle is crisp and nutty brown. Set waffle directly on oven rack to keep it warm and crisp. Repeat with remaining batter, holding waffles in oven; do not stack. When all waffles are cooked, serve immediately.

Makes 4 to 5 (8-inch) waffles

Note: A required rest in the oven helps keep waffles crisp and allows one to make a large batch.

Apricot Bellinis

- 2 (15-ounce) cans apricot halves, drained
- 2 (15-ounce) cans apricot nectar
- 1/2 cup sugar
- Crushed ice
- 1 (750-milliliter) bottle sparkling wine or champagne, chilled

Process half of each of first 3 ingredients in blender until smooth, stopping to scrape down sides. Repeat with remaining apricot halves, nectar and sugar. Serve over crushed ice with sparkling wine. Garnish with mint sprigs if desired.

Serves 8 (1-cup each)

Note: 2 (12-ounce) cans ginger ale or lemon-lime soda can be substituted for wine.

Bacon and Egg Pie

An ideal dish to serve for a weekend brunch.

- 1 1/2 teaspoons unsalted butter
- 8 ounces thickly sliced bacon
- 4 ounces mushrooms, cleaned and quartered
- 1 red, yellow or orange bell pepper, seeded, ribs removed and diced
- 4 ounces soft goat cheese
- 1/2 cup fresh grated Parmesan cheese
- 1 tablespoon fresh thyme leaves
- 5 large eggs
- 1 1/2 cups heavy cream
- Kosher salt and fresh ground black pepper

Preheat oven to 325 degrees. Generously butter a 10-inch pie dish. Cook bacon until very crisp. Remove and drain on paper towels. Pour off all but 2 tablespoons of bacon fat.

Return pan to medium-high heat and add mushrooms to drippings. Cook until well browned (about 4 minutes). Spread mushrooms in prepared pie dish. Crumble bacon and arrange over mushrooms. Add pepper, cheeses and thyme.

Beat eggs and cream and season with salt and pepper. Pour egg mixture over bacon-vegetable mixture. Bake until egg pie is set and deep golden brown (about 1 hour). Remove from oven and let sit for 10 minutes. Slice into wedges. Serve warm or at room temperature.

Serves 6 to 8

Note: Pre-cooked bacon may be used. Bake pie the night before and warm in oven, on low heat, before serving.

Simple Basil Strata

1 cup low-fat or fat-free milk
1/2 cup dry white wine
1 French baguette sliced 1/2-inch thick on the diagonal
8 ounces thinly sliced Prosciutto, cut into pieces
2 cups packed baby spinach
1 pound sliced Provolone cheese
3 ripe tomatoes, skinned and thinly sliced
1/2 cup prepared pesto
4 eggs
Salt and pepper to taste

The night before serving, mix milk and wine together and briefly soak bread in liquid and squeeze out most of the liquid. Place one layer of bread in a 12-inch round baking dish or other casserole dish. Layer with Prosciutto, spinach, Provolone and tomato slices and drizzle with 2 – 3 tablespoons pesto. Repeat layers starting with bread and ending with pesto until dish is full. Beat eggs lightly with salt and pepper and pour gently over strata. Cover with plastic wrap and chill overnight. Remove dish from refrigerator and bring to room temperature. Bake in 350 degree oven 45-60 minutes until strata is puffy and browned. Serve immediately.

Serves 6 to 8

Savory Rosemary Breakfast Strata

5 cups cubed day old bread
4 links Italian turkey sausage, casings removed, browned and crumbled
1/4 cup chopped sun-dried tomatoes packed in oil, reserving oil
1/2 cup chopped onion
1 to 2 tablespoons chopped fresh rosemary
4 - 6 ounces Monterey Jack cheese, shredded (1 to 1 1/2 cups)
6 large eggs
1 1/2 cups milk
1 teaspoon salt
1/4 teaspoon freshly ground pepper
1 teaspoon dry mustard
1/4 teaspoon nutmeg (optional)

Prepare a 9-inch square baking dish. Place bread cubes in casserole and spread sausage evenly over bread. Pour 1 tablespoon reserved sun-dried tomato oil into skillet, add onions and sauté until tender. Add tomatoes and rosemary, stirring until blended. Place onion mixture over sausage and cover with cheese. Whisk eggs, milk, salt, pepper, dry mustard and nutmeg until well blended. Pour egg mixture over casserole and cover. Refrigerate 8-10 hours or overnight. Bring to room temperature before baking. Bake at 350 degrees 30-45 minutes until set.

Note: Add mushrooms if desired.

Honeydew Mimosas

- 1/2 medium honeydew melon (about 4 cups), cubed
- 1 cup crushed ice
- 1 tablespoon sugar
- 1 (750 ml) bottle sparkling wine, chilled
- Lime wedge, garnish

Combine first 3 ingredients in blender. Process until smooth, pour into pitcher and add sparkling wine. Garnish with lime wedges.

Serves 6 (8-ounces) each

Poached Eggs with Asparagus, Prosciutto and Chive Oil

- 1/2 cup extra virgin olive oil
- 1/4 cup fresh chopped chives
- 1 teaspoon fresh lemon juice
- 1/4 teaspoon lemon zest
- 6-12 large eggs
- 2 pounds medium asparagus spears, trimmed
- 1-3 tablespoons olive oil
- 3 ounces prosciutto, thinly sliced

Blend extra virgin olive oil, chives and lemon juice in blender or processor until smooth. Stir in lemon zest and season to taste with salt and pepper. Cover and chill. Return to room temperature before using.

Poach eggs, being careful not to break yolks.

Preheat broiler. Spread asparagus in single layer on rimmed baking sheet. Drizzle with olive oil, salt and pepper, turning to coat. Broil 6 minutes, turn asparagus and broil until crisp-tender and beginning to brown, about 6 minutes longer. Divide asparagus among 6 plates and cover with prosciutto.

Place 1 or 2 eggs on top of prosciutto.

Drizzle chive oil over and around each serving. Pass remaining chive oil.

Serves 6

Firehouse Omelet

12 eggs
1 cup rice, cooked in 2 cups water
4 ounces butter, melted
1 cup ham, cubed
1 pound small curd cottage cheese
1 (1.8-ounce) package leek soup mix
1 teaspoon onion salt
1/2 teaspoon black pepper
1 (10-ounce) package frozen spinach, thawed, drained and squeezed of water
1/2 cup Parmesan cheese

Preheat oven to 325 degrees

In a large bowl beat 9 eggs; add cooked rice, melted butter, ham, cottage cheese, soup mix, spices and spinach and mix together. Spread 1/4 cup Parmesan on bottom of 9 x 13-inch baking dish and cover with rice and cottage cheese mixture. Beat remaining eggs and pour over top of mixture. Sprinkle with remaining Parmesan.

Bake 40 – 50 minutes, remove and let cool 15 – 20 minutes. Consistency should be similar to quiche without crust.

Serves 6 to 8

Note: May be refrigerated, covered, several hours or overnight. Bring to room temperature before baking. Sausage, salami or bacon may be used. Omit meat for a vegetarian dish.

Fried Eggs on Toast with Pepper Jack and Avocado

3 tablespoons butter, room temperature
4 large eggs
Salt and pepper
4 slices hot pepper Monterey Jack cheese
Thick slices country bread
1 avocado, peeled, pitted, sliced
Chopped cilantro

Preheat broiler. Melt 1 tablespoon butter in a heavy, large ovenproof skillet over medium heat. Crack eggs into skillet; salt and pepper eggs and cook until egg whites are set, about 2 minutes. Top each egg with a cheese slice. Broil until cheese melts, about 1 minute.

Toast and butter bread, top with eggs and avocado slices. Sprinkle with cilantro.

Serves 4

Baked Eggs with Italian Sausage and Potatoes

2 pounds Idaho russet potatoes
1 1/2 pounds lean Italian sausage, casings removed
1 large onion, finely chopped
2 tablespoons extra virgin olive oil
Salt and freshly ground pepper
8 eggs
Toast
Hot sauce

Preheat oven to 375 degrees. Cook potatoes with skins on until easily pierced with fork, peel and cut into 3/4- inch pieces.

Using a 12-inch cast iron or non-stick skillet cook sausage over medium heat, breaking up large pieces, until lightly browned and thoroughly cooked, about 8 minutes. Add onion and cook until softened, about 5 minutes. Set sausage mixture aside, wipe out skillet.

Heat oil and add potatoes, season with salt and pepper and cook over moderate heat until golden and crispy, about 6 minutes. Stir in sausage mixture. Mixture can be placed in baking dish or left in an oven-safe skillet. Using a ladle, make 8 indentations in potato-sausage mixture, about one inch apart; crack an egg into each indentation. Bake in middle of oven about 12 minutes, or until eggs are set.

Spinach & Sun-Dried Tomato Frittata

Vegetable oil cooking spray
2 teaspoons olive oil
1 small shallot, chopped
1 cup packed fresh spinach, chopped
4 whole eggs
4 egg whites
8 sun-dried tomato halves, chopped
1/2 cup grated Asiago cheese
2 tablespoons chopped fresh basil
1/4 teaspoon salt
1/8 teaspoon freshly ground black pepper

Preheat oven to 425 degrees. Coat 9-inch glass pie dish with cooking spray. Set aside.

Heat oil in a large pan over medium heat. Cook shallot until soft but not brown, 2 to 3 minutes. Add spinach; cook 2 to 3 minutes. Remove from heat. Lightly whisk eggs and egg whites in a bowl. Stir in tomatoes, cheese, basil, spinach mixture, salt and pepper. Spoon into pie dish; bake until firm in the center, 15 to 18 minutes.

Serves 6 to 8

Note: This can be prepared in a frittata pan on stove top.

Brown Butter Crepes with Nutella and Jam

2 tablespoons unsalted butter, more for cooking
1 large egg
1 large egg yolk
1 cup half-and-half
3/4 cup all-purpose flour
Salt and freshly ground pepper
1/2 cup strawberry or peach jam
1/2 cup Nutella

Preheat oven to 225 degrees. Brown 2 tablespoons butter over moderately high heat, about 4 minutes; let cool.

Whisk egg and yolk with half-and-half; whisk in flour and browned butter. Season with salt and pepper.

Place a non-stick crepe pan over high heat. When hot add a scant 1/4 cup of batter, swirling to coat bottom of pan. Cook until crepe is browned around edges and top is set, about 45 seconds. Flip crepe and cook until underside is lightly browned, about 30 seconds longer. Repeat, adding butter as needed, making about 8 crepes.

Spread each crepe with a tablespoon of jam and fold into quarters. Place in a small baking dish, overlapping slightly. Bake 10 minutes, until crepes are heated through. Heat Nutella in microwave on high power, in 20-second bursts, until runny. Drizzle Nutella over warm crepes and serve.

Serves 4

Note: Crepes can be prepared with different fillings. For a savory dish fill with Gruyère cheese and sautéed vegetables such as mushrooms and onions. For a fruity version fill crepes with strawberries and blueberries and top with melted chocolate or powdered sugar.

Boozy Cherry Tomatoes

2 pints cherry or grape tomatoes
1 1/2 cups vodka
3 tablespoons sea salt
2 tablespoons chopped basil
Fresh cracked pepper

Gently pierce each tomato in several places. Place tomatoes in glass bowl and cover with vodka. Marinate for at least 4 hours at room temperature; turn occasionally. Drain tomatoes, generously salt and pepper and serve with toothpicks. Save vodka for bloody Marys.

Breakfast Panini

- 6 slices bacon
- 6 eggs
- 1/3 cup milk, half-and-half or light cream
- Salt and pepper
- 6 Ciabatta rolls, split
- 2 tablespoons snipped fresh basil and/or oregano
- 4 ounces Fontina cheese, thinly sliced
- 1/2 cup roasted red peppers

Cook bacon until crisp, drain, reserving 1 tablespoon drippings.

Combine eggs, milk, salt and pepper. Cook mixture in drippings over medium heat, without stirring, until mixture begins to set on bottom and around edges.

With spatula, lift and fold mixture so uncooked egg flows underneath. When cooked through but still glossy and moist, spoon onto rolls. Top with herbs, bacon, cheese and peppers.

Cook on panini sandwich grill or grill pan until rolls are browned.

Serves 6

Egg and Sausage Breakfast Pizza

- 1 loaf Ciabatta bread
- 1 cup chopped green onions
- 8 tablespoons olive oil
- Salt and pepper
- 8 (1-ounce) slices pepper Jack cheese
- 1 pound sweet Italian sausage
- 8 large eggs

Preheat oven to 450 degrees. Cut bread in half horizontally and place cut side up on two baking sheets. Mix onions with 6 tablespoons oil and season with salt and pepper. Reserve 2 tablespoons onion oil and spread remaining oil over bread; top with cheese.

Sauté sausage over medium high heat until cooked through, breaking up with a spoon, about 7 minutes. Divide sausage between bread halves. Bake until cheese melts and bread begins to crisp, about 10 minutes.

While pizzas are baking, heat 1 tablespoon oil in each of 2 large skillets over medium high heat. Cook seasoned eggs, about 3-4 minutes, or to taste.

Arrange 4 eggs atop each pizza. Spoon reserved onion oil over eggs. Cut each pizza between eggs into 4 pieces.

Serves 8

Note: Farm to Market Ciabatta suggested or substitute English muffins.

Scones

- 3 cups all-purpose flour
- 1 tablespoon baking powder
- 1/2 pound unsalted butter, room temperature
- 1/4 cup plus 2 tablespoons sugar
- 3 large eggs
- 1/3 cup buttermilk or plain yogurt

Preheat oven to 350 degrees. Combine flour and baking powder. In large bowl beat butter until creamy, add sugar and beat 3-5 minutes until pale and fluffy. Add eggs, one at a time, beating after each addition. Scrape sides of bowl; reduce speed to low and add buttermilk or yogurt; mix only until blended. Scoop 1/3 cupfuls of dough onto cookie sheet, placing 2-inches apart. Loosely cover dough with plastic wrap and refrigerate about 45 minutes. Bake about 13 minutes then reduce heat to 325 degrees and bake 13 minutes longer or until golden brown.

Variations: Add 1/2 cup small semisweet chocolate chips or currants, 1 teaspoon cinnamon and 1/2 teaspoon nutmeg. Drop onto cookie sheet by the tablespoon.

Makes 13 large or 27 small

Country Fair Egg Bread

- 2 packages yeast
- 1/2 cup lukewarm water
- 1 1/2 cups warm milk
- 8 tablespoons butter
- 1 teaspoon salt
- 1/2 cup sugar
- 2 eggs, beaten
- 5 1/2-6 cups flour
- Egg wash, optional

Preheat oven to 425 degrees. Dissolve yeast in water. Pour milk over butter, salt and sugar; mix. Mix in yeast and eggs. Gradually add flour. Mix in a stand mixer or by hand until dough is smooth and elastic. Place dough in bowl and let rise for an hour. Divide dough into three equal parts. Braid each loaf of dough and place on baking sheets or place in 9 x 5 loaf pans. Brush with egg wash, if desired. Place in oven and turn temperature to 350 degrees. Bake approximately 30 minutes. Can brush with melted butter after baked.

Light Banana Bread

1 cup sugar
1/4 cup light butter (Blue Bonnet suggested)
1 2/3 cups mashed ripe bananas
1/4 cup fat-free milk
1/4 cup low-fat sour cream
2 large eggs (whites only may be used)
2 cups all-purpose flour or 1 cup whole wheat and 1 cup white
1 teaspoon baking soda
1/2 teaspoon salt
Cooking spray

Preheat oven to 350 degrees. Prepare four 5 x 2 1/2-inch mini-loaf pans or one 9-inch loaf pan. Beat sugar and butter at medium speed until well blended. Add banana, milk, sour cream and eggs. Beat well. Sift together flour, baking soda and salt. Add flour mixture to sugar mixture and beat until just blended. Spoon batter into pans and bake small pans 45 minutes or large pan 1 hour and 10 minutes. Cool 10 minutes in pans then turn onto rack to finish cooling.

Very Lemon Bread

1/3 cup butter, melted
1 cup sugar
3 tablespoons lemon extract
2 eggs, lightly beaten
1 1/2 cups flour
1 teaspoon baking powder
1 teaspoon salt
1/2 cup milk
2 tablespoons lemon zest
1/2 cup chopped pecans

Glaze
1/4 cup lemon juice
1/2 cup sugar

Preheat oven to 350 degrees. Mix butter, sugar, lemon extract and eggs; in a separate bowl sift flour with baking powder and salt. Add flour mixture to butter mixture, alternating with milk to blend. Fold in lemon zest and pecans.

Pour batter into greased and floured 9 x 5-inch loaf pan. Bake 1 hour or until a toothpick tests clean. While bread is still warm drizzle with lemon glaze. Cool, then wrap in foil; store 1 day before slicing.

Wheat Germ Zucchini Bread

3 eggs, beaten
1 cup sugar
1 cup brown sugar
1 cup cooking oil
3 teaspoons maple flavoring
2 cups coarsely shredded zucchini, peeled or not peeled, packed
2 teaspoons soda
2 teaspoons salt
1/2 teaspoon baking powder
1/2 cup regular wheat germ
2 1/2 cups unsifted flour
1 cup pecans or walnuts
1/3 cup sesame seeds (optional)

Preheat oven to 350 degrees. Beat together eggs, sugars, oil and maple flavoring until foamy. Stir in zucchini. Mix together soda, baking powder, salt, wheat germ and flour. Add to egg mixture. Add nuts. Spoon batter into 2 greased and floured 9 x 5-inch loaf pans and sprinkle with sesame seeds, if desired. Bake about 1 hour or until toothpick tests clean.

Cool in pans 10 minutes and turn to cool on racks.

Note: Test with a toothpick after 45 or 50 minutes of baking.

Oatmeal Blueberry Muffins

1 1/4 cups quick-cook oatmeal
1 1/4 cups flour
1/3 cup sugar
1 tablespoon baking powder
1/2 teaspoon salt
1 cup milk
1/4 cup oil
1 egg
3/4 cup blueberries
2 tablespoons sugar
2 teaspoons cinnamon

Preheat oven to 425 degrees. Lightly grease a 12-cup muffin pan. Combine oatmeal, flour, sugar, baking powder and salt. In a separate bowl combine milk, oil and egg. Combine two mixtures, stir until just moistened. Fold in blueberries and spoon into muffin cups. Mix sugar and cinnamon and sprinkle 1 teaspoon over top of batter.

Bake 13 minutes or until a toothpick tests clean.

Note: May be frozen

Cranberry Spice Muffins

3 cups flour
1 tablespoon baking powder
1/2 teaspoon baking soda
1/2 teaspoon salt
1 tablespoon cinnamon
2 teaspoons ginger
1 1/4 cups skim milk
3 large eggs
1/2 pound butter, melted and cooled
1 1/2 cups craisins
3/4 cup brown sugar
3/4 cup sugar
1/2 cup coarsely broken pecans

Preheat oven to 375 degrees. Sift together flour, baking powder, baking soda, salt, cinnamon and ginger. Add milk, eggs and melted butter, stir to combine. Add craisins, both sugars and pecans, mixing until combined. Do not beat. Line 18 muffin cups with paper liners and spoon batter to top of liners. Bake on middle rack of oven 20-25 minutes or until toothpick tests clean.

Bishop's Bread

If your family does not like fruit cake try this instead.

3 eggs
1 cup sugar
1 1/2 cups flour
1 1/2 teaspoons baking powder
1/4 teaspoon salt
1 cup nuts
1 cup dates
1 cup maraschino cherries
1/4 pound bar sweet chocolate, broken into fair sized pieces

Preheat oven to 325 degrees. Beat eggs and combine with sugar. Mix flour, baking powder and salt; sift this over nuts, dates, cherries and chocolate. Add to first mixture. Grease 9 x 5-inch loaf pan thoroughly and line bottom with greased parchment paper. Pour in batter and bake approximately 1 hour and 20 minutes. Cool and slice very thin for serving.

Honey Wheat Bread with Apricot Cranberry Butter

Bread

1 tablespoon yeast
2 1/2 cups plus 1/8 cup water
3/8 cup honey
2 1/2 cups all-purpose flour or bread flour
3 tablespoons soft butter or canola oil
1/2 tablespoon salt
3 tablespoons wheat gluten, optional
2 1/2 cups whole wheat flour

Place yeast in bowl of large food processor or stand mixer fitted with dough hook. Add water and honey, blend briefly and let rest 2-3 minutes. Add white flour and mix to blend. Add butter or oil and mix thoroughly. Add salt, wheat gluten and whole wheat flour and process well. Allow mixer or processor to knead dough 5-10 minutes until elastic. Turn out into oiled bowl, cover and set aside to double in bulk, approximately 1- 1 1/2 hours. Punch down dough and turn over several times; cover and let rise again about 1 hour. Form dough into 2 equal loaves. (May be baked in oval, round or loaf pans). Cover a third time and let rise until double. Bake in 350 degrees preheated oven approximately 45 minutes. Loaves should be lightly brown and sound hollow when thumped on bottom.

Apricot Cranberry Butter

1/4 cup apricot preserves
1/4 cup white wine
8 tablespoons butter, softened
1/3 cup combination of chopped dried apricots and cranberries

Microwave dried fruit in wine 2 minutes on high. Cover and let rest a few minutes for fruit to absorb wine. Drain any remaining wine and let cool. Blend all ingredients thoroughly. Chill and serve with breads.

Variation: Roll dough into large rectangle (24 x 18-inches or so) and spread with 2 cups chopped pecans, 2 tablespoons cinnamon and 3/4 cup brown sugar. Roll dough, jelly roll fashion into a long tube. Bring ends together to make large circle. Brush with melted butter and bake 45 minutes until brown.

Soups & Salads

Menu Ideas

Sweet Plum-Tomato Soup with Goat Cheese and Chive 54
Spinach Salad 62
Cinnamon Honey Fruit Salad 67
Lacy Oatmeal Cookies 146

or Hearty Tortilla Soup 58
CCVI's Favorite Caesar Salad 65
Cranberry Apple Dessert . . . . (*Then and Now*) 222
or Grand Finale Apple Cake 144

Soups & Salads

Mulligatawny Soup

3 cups chopped vegetables (mixture of onions, carrots, celery, parsnips, mushrooms)
6 cups broth (meat, vegetable or chicken)
1 teaspoon finely chopped garlic
2 teaspoons ground coriander
1/4 teaspoon black pepper
2 tablespoons light vegetable oil
1/2 cup finely chopped onions
4 teaspoons curry powder
3 tablespoons flour
1/2 cup heavy cream
Salt to taste
1 tablespoon ground coriander

Place vegetables, broth, garlic, coriander and black pepper in a 3-quart pan. Bring to a boil. Reduce heat and simmer, covered, 45 minutes or until vegetables are soft. (Can refrigerate, when cooled, until next day.)

Puree soup in a blender or food processor. Return soup to pan and bring to a gentle simmer.

While soup is simmering, fry onions in oil until a caramel brown (about 10 minutes), stirring constantly to prevent burning. Add curry powder and flour and cook mixture for 1 minute, stirring rapidly. Turn off heat and add mixture to soup, stirring constantly to prevent lumping. Simmer until soup is thickened (about 2 minutes).

Note: Soup may be made up to this point and set aside, covered, for several hours or refrigerated for up to 3 days, or frozen. Defrost and heat thoroughly before proceeding to next step.

To serve: Stir in cream, salt and ground coriander. Simmer over low heat until warmed through.

Serves 6 to 10 as first course

Light Split Pea Soup

1 pound split peas
1 ham bone
2 quarts boiling water
1 carrot, sliced
1 stalk celery, sliced
1 medium onion, diced
Pinch of ground cloves
Salt and pepper to taste

Rinse and sort peas; drain. Rinse ham bone; add bone and onion to boiling water. Add peas and other vegetables. Boil moderately fast 2 1/2 hours. More water may be added during cooking if necessary. Stir occasionally to prevent sticking. Remove ham bone. Serve hot with diced ham bits as garnish.

Serves: 10 or more if first course

Cheesy Zucchini Soup

2 medium zucchini, grated
2 medium carrots, grated
1 medium onion, chopped
4 ounces margarine or butter
4 tablespoons flour
2 (13 1/2-ounce) cans chicken broth
4 ounces grated Monterey Jack cheese
1 cup milk
Salt and pepper to taste

Place grated zucchini in a colander; sprinkle with salt and let sit for 30 minutes. Press to drain well. In a soup pot sauté grated and chopped vegetables in butter until slightly limp. Stir in flour and cook over low heat 5 minutes, stirring constantly. Slowly add chicken broth and stir until smooth. Add grated cheese and stir until melted. Add milk; season to taste. Do not boil.

Serves 6

Spinach Soup

2 pounds spinach, large stems removed
4 cups chicken stock
2 carrots, large slices
2 potatoes, quartered
1 small onion, chopped
1 cup milk, any kind
4 ounces cream cheese, cubed
Ground white pepper
Dash of nutmeg
Salt, if desired

Cook spinach 5 minutes; drain and set aside. Cook carrots, potatoes and onion in chicken stock. Place everything in blender, add milk and cheese, puree. Add white pepper, nutmeg and salt to taste.

Note: Garnishing with hard boiled egg and shrimp adds a festive touch.

Serves 6 to 8

Tip
If soup or vegetables are over-salted, add cut raw potatoes and discard once they have cooked and absorbed salt.

Easy Delicious Vegetable Soup

Makes a Huge Pot of Soup.

- 1 tablespoon oil
- 1 onion, chopped
- 2 pounds lean stew meat, cubed
- 2 garlic cloves, minced
- 2 (46-ounce) cans V-8 juice
- 2 (14-ounce) cans beef broth
- 1 (28-ounce) bag frozen diced potatoes
- 2 (16-ounce) bags frozen mixed vegetables
- 1 (14.5-ounce) can whole tomatoes, chopped
- 1 1/2 teaspoons brown sugar
- 3 stalks celery, diced
- Chopped parsley

Sauté onion in oil. Add meat and garlic; brown all. Add all ingredients but parsley. Bring to a boil and simmer for at least one hour; longer is better.

Garnish with chopped parsley.

Sweet Plum-Tomato Soup with Goat Cheese and Chive

Todd Schutte . . . Happy Soup Eater 549 Gillis, Kansas City, MO
Order on line at www.HappySoupEater.com

- 1 ounce olive oil
- 1 medium onion, finely chopped
- 1 pound plums, pits removed
- 2 pounds tomatoes, peeled, cored, seeded
- 3 ounces tomato juice
- 20 ounces chicken stock
- 1 sprig thyme
- 1 tablespoon sugar
- Salt and pepper

Garnish: sliced plums, fresh goat cheese, snipped chives and blossoms

Heat oil and sauté onions until soft but not brown. Add remaining ingredients and bring to a boil. Lower heat and simmer 15 minutes. Cool and remove thyme. Puree in blender and chill. Check the seasoning and serve with garnish.

Serves 4 to 6 (1-cup serving)

Creamy Tomato Basil Soup

- 1 medium yellow onion, minced
- 3 large garlic cloves, minced
- 1 tablespoon olive oil
- 2 cups chicken stock
- 2 ounces fresh basil, chopped fine
- 2 (20-ounce) cans tomato puree
- 2 (15-ounce) cans tomato sauce
- 2 tablespoons sugar
- Salt and white pepper to taste
- 1/2 cup unsalted butter, cubed
- 1/2 pint heavy whipping cream

Sauté onion and garlic in olive oil until translucent. Add chicken stock and basil. Bring to a simmer. Add tomato puree and sauce and bring to a simmer. Add sugar, salt and pepper and simmer for 10 minutes. Can be refrigerated at this point. When ready to serve, puree ingredients in blender or food processor. Place in cooking pot and warm. Whisk in butter and heavy cream. Bring just to a simmer and serve.

Serves 8 to 10

Gazpacho

Andrew Sloan, Room 39 at Mission Farms
10561 Mission Road, Leawood, Kansas

- 5 pounds local tomatoes, core and quarter
- 2 cucumbers, peel, seed and cut into 1-inch pieces
- 1 large yellow onion, diced
- 1 sprig fresh oregano
- 1 tablespoon chopped fresh basil
- 1/4 cup sherry vinegar
- 1 cup Pellegrino (soda water)
- Salt and pepper
- Garnish: small croutons, extra virgin olive oil

Combine all ingredients except Pellegrino, salt and pepper. Using a food processor or blender, process mixture and pour into a plastic container. Add salt and pepper to taste and chill 3 hours. Before serving add Pellegrino and pour into chilled bowls. Garnish with small croutons and extra virgin olive oil.

Serves 8 to 10

Tip
Mix 1 (26-ounce) jar of Classico spaghetti sauce (your choice of flavor) with an equal amount of milk for quick and tasty tomato soup.

Chilled Corn Soup with Jalapeno Crème Fraiche

Andrew Sloan, Room 39 at Mission Farms
10561Mission Road, Leawood, Kansas

2 tablespoons butter
6 ears corn, kernels cut off
2 onions, sliced
2 ribs celery, sliced
2 leeks, sliced
2 potatoes, sliced
4-5 cloves garlic
2 quarts vegetable stock
Salt and pepper
1 cup heavy cream
2 tablespoons buttermilk
1 tablespoon heavy cream
1 jalapeno

In large stainless steel pot melt butter over low-medium heat. Add corn, onions, celery, leeks, potatoes and garlic. Sauté slowly until vegetables are soft, about 10 minutes. Add stock and bring to boil, reduce to simmer. Cook 10 minutes or until potatoes are cooked. Puree in a blender, run through a fine mesh strainer and chill overnight or at least 3 hours.

Crème fraiche: heat cream to 90-100 degrees. Pour cream into a clean container and add buttermilk, cover and let sit at room temperature for 24 hours. Refrigerate; may be used for two weeks.

Jalapeno crème fraiche: Puree jalapeno with cream and fold into crème fraiche.

Top each serving with a dollop of jalapeno crème fraiche.

Serves 8 to 10

Artichoke Mushroom Soup

2 tablespoons chopped onion
1 cup thinly sliced fresh mushrooms
3 tablespoons butter
2 tablespoons flour
1-1/2 cups chicken stock
2-1/2 cups half-and-half
1 (13.25 ounces) can artichoke hearts in water, drained and chopped
Salt, as desired
Cayenne pepper, as desired
Beau Monde seasoning, as desired

In a soup pot, cook onions and mushroom in butter for about 5 minutes. Stir in flour and cook slowly for 2 minutes. Slowly add stock and half-and-half. Cook over low heat, whisking until thickened. Stir in artichoke hearts and season to taste.

Serves 4 to 6 main course

Clam Chowder

8 slices bacon
1 cup finely chopped onion
1 cup finely chopped celery
3 (6-1/2 ounce) cans chopped clams, drained; reserve juice
2 cups low sodium, low-fat chicken broth
2 large turnips, peeled and cubed (can use 3 potatoes)
1/2 teaspoon pepper
1 teaspoon dried thyme
Salt
2 tablespoons cornstarch
1/4 cup water
2 cups heavy cream

Fry bacon and set aside, reserving bacon grease. Sauté onion and celery in bacon grease until soft. Place into larger pot.

Add clam juice, chicken broth, turnips (or potatoes), pepper, thyme and salt. Cover and cook over medium heat, stirring occasionally, until turnips (or potatoes) are soft, about 15 minutes.

Stir cornstarch into water; add to soup. Heat just until bubbly and slightly thickened.

Remove from heat and stir in heavy cream and clams.

Crumble bacon and add to soup. Reheat over low heat before serving.

Serves 6 to 8

Tortellini Soup

1 pound ground beef, browned
2 garlic cloves, sliced
1 1/2 tablespoons olive oil
1 (14.5-ounce) can French cut green beans, drained
1 (10-ounce) can Ro-Tel tomatoes
1 (14.5-ounce) can diced or crushed tomatoes (Italian style)
1 (10.5-ounce) can low sodium French onion soup
1 (14-ounce) can beef broth
2 cups water
1 (14-ounce) bag frozen cheese tortellini

Sauté garlic cloves in olive oil; add browned ground beef. Add green beans, both cans tomatoes, onion soup, beef broth and water. Simmer 1 hour. Add tortellini and simmer 1/2 hour.

Note: All or half of the soup can be frozen before adding the tortellini.

Serves 10

Hearty Tortilla Soup

2 cloves garlic, chopped
1 onion, chopped
1/2 green pepper, chopped
2 stalks celery, chopped
1 tablespoon olive oil
1 (15-ounce) can crushed tomatoes
4 cups chicken broth
2 (4-ounce) cans chopped green chiles
1 (10 3/4-ounce) can cream of mushroom soup
2 cups cooked, chopped chicken or turkey
1 teaspoon oregano
1 teaspoon salt
1 teaspoon pepper
2 teaspoons chili powder
1 teaspoon cumin

Garnish
Shredded cheddar cheese
Diced avocado
Crushed tortilla chips

Sauté onion, green pepper, celery and garlic in olive oil until soft. Add remaining ingredients and stir well. Bring to a boil. Reduce heat and simmer for at least one hour.

Serves 4 to 6

Jim's Lentil Soup

Great for a tailgate party.

2 1-pound packages of lentils
1 (12-ounce) package salt pork
8 garlic cloves
8 large carrots, peeled
10 stalks celery
2 medium onions
1 leek, white part only, chopped
1 (14-ounce) can chicken broth

Cover lentils with water and soak overnight.

Dice salt pork into medium-size pieces. Place in bottom of a large stockpot (approximately 12 quarts). Heat pork on low until it starts to brown. Add cruschetta (see below) to pot.

Sauté cruschetta until onions are clear. Drain lentils and add to pot. Add chicken broth. Add water until pot is 1/2 full. Cook and simmer for at least 4 hours. Add water to thin, if desired. Soup can be frozen

Cruschetta
Chop garlic, carrots, celery, onions and leek into fine pieces and combine. A food processor can be used.

Serves 20

Florence's Matzo Ball Soup

Florence claimed the secret of her light matzo balls was the "seltzer."

- 8 chicken breast halves, skinned (leave on bone)
- 2 large onions, peeled and left whole
- 3 parsnips, peeled and left whole
- 12 carrots, peeled and trimmed
- 3 stalks celery
- 3 sprigs parsley
- 5 chicken bouillon cubes (Telma brand found in Kosher area of store)
- 2 tablespoons sugar
- 1 tablespoons salt
- Pepper, to taste

Fill a large stockpot (approximately 12 quarts) 3/4 full of water and bring to a boil. Add chicken. Scoop off white froth. Add vegetables, bouillon cubes, salt and pepper. Cook 3 hours.

Matzo Balls

- 1 cup matzo meal (Kosher section of store)
- 4 eggs
- 1/3 cup vegetable oil
- 1/2 cup seltzer

Mix eggs and vegetable oil with a fork. Add matzo meal; blend. Add seltzer. Refrigerate 1/2 hour. Wet hands in cold water. Roll ingredients into balls (like a meatball). Place in soup that is simmering. Turn matzo balls after 1/2 hour.

Discard onions, celery, parsley and parsnips. Cut up chicken, slice carrots and return to soup. Soup can be frozen without matzo balls. You can use only half the cooked chicken if you choose. The remainder makes an excellent chicken salad.

Can place cooked Ditali pasta in bottom of each bowl before serving.

Serves 10 to 12

Southwest Style White Chili

5 cups water
1 teaspoon lemon pepper
4 teaspoons cumin seed
1 pound boneless, skinless chicken breasts
2 garlic cloves, minced
1 cup chopped onion

Combine first 4 ingredients in a large stock pot.

Cook until chicken breasts are tender. Remove chicken and reserve broth.

Cool chicken and cut into small pieces. Spray a skillet with oil, add minced garlic and sauté 1 minute. Add to broth. Sauté chopped onion until tender and add to broth.

Add to broth

1 (16-ounce) package frozen shoepeg corn
2 (4-ounce) cans chopped green chiles with juice
1 tablespoon ground cumin
3 tablespoons fresh lime juice
1 tablespoon chicken bouillon granules
3 (15-ounce) cans Great Northern Beans with juice

Cook until flavors mix, about 15 minutes. Flavor will improve the longer chili sets.

Serve with toppings such as grated Monterey Jack cheese, sour cream, salsa and crushed corn chips.

Serves 15

Tip

To remove burnt on food from a skillet or pan add powdered dishwasher soap and enough water to cover the bottom of the pan. Bring to a boil, this will help release the food.

Tasty Black Bean Soup

- 1 teaspoon olive oil
- 3/4 cup chopped onions
- 3 (15-ounce) cans black beans
- 2 (14-ounce) cans chicken broth
- 1 (15-ounce) can corn, drained (or frozen)
- 1 (14.5-ounce) can Mexican-style stewed tomatoes, chopped
- 1/4 cup bottled salsa
- 3 bay leaves
- 1 teaspoon minced garlic
- 1 teaspoon dried thyme
- 1 teaspoon balsamic vinegar
- 1/2 teaspoon ground cumin

Heat oil in a 4 1/2 quart soup pot over medium heat. Add onions and cook until slightly browned, stirring occasionally. Pour 1 can of beans with liquid into a large bowl. Using the back of a serving spoon, mash beans against sides and bottom of bowl until they are broken up and pasty (can pulse in a food processor). Increase heat to high and add chicken broth, mashed beans and 2 cans whole beans with liquid. Stir well.

Drain corn and add it to pot, then add tomatoes, salsa, bay leaves, garlic, thyme, vinegar and cumin. Cover pot and bring to a boil. Reduce heat to low and simmer to blend flavors for about 8 minutes, stirring often to prevent sticking. Remove from heat and serve.

For a thicker soup, stir 2 tablespoons cornstarch into a little water and add with whole beans.

Serves 8

Tip

Put onion in freezer for a few minutes before cutting. Leave the root end intact until last.

Baked Tortellini Soup

Ricki Creamer of Red Cedar Country Gardens
Adapted from Colorado Collage Cookbook

1 1/2 pounds Italian sausage links
1 cup chopped onion
1 teaspoon minced garlic
1/4 teaspoon freshly ground black pepper
2 tablespoons olive oil
4 cups beef broth
2 cups water
1 1/2 teaspoons Italian seasoning
1 1/2 cups peeled and thinly sliced carrots
1 (16-ounce) can whole peeled tomatoes
1 (15-ounce) can kidney beans, drained and rinsed
1 (6-ounce) can pitted, sliced ripe olives, drained or oil-cured olives
2 cups diced zucchini
1 (16-ounce) bag tri-color cheese tortellini cooked al dente and drained
Freshly grated Parmesan cheese

Preheat oven to 400 degrees. In roasting pan, combine sausage, onion, garlic and pepper. Add olive oil and toss to coat. Roast, uncovered, stirring occasionally, 20-30 minutes, until sausage is browned. Remove from oven. Reduce temperature to 325 degrees.

Drain grease from sausage and cut into 1/4-inch slices. Return to roasting pan. Add beef broth, water, Italian seasoning and carrots. Cover and return to oven. Bake 30 minutes, until sausage is tender. Remove from oven and stir in tomatoes with juice, beans, olives and zucchini. Bake 15-20 minutes. Add tortellini and bake 5 minutes longer. Ladle into warmed bowls and garnish with Parmesan.

Serves 8

Spinach Salad

2 tablespoons cider vinegar
1/2 cup mayonnaise
1 tablespoon honey
4 slices cooked bacon, chopped (optional)
2 tablespoons chopped scallion or sweet onion

Mix all together. Keeps well in the refrigerator.

Serve over spinach with chopped eggs, mushrooms, more bacon or ingredients to your taste.

Tangy Bayside Salad

2 tablespoons butter
1/4 cup chopped pecans
2 cups torn romaine lettuce
1 (5-ounce) package spring mix salad greens
1/4 sweet red onion, thinly sliced
1/4 cup crumbled blue cheese
4 slices bacon, cooked until crisp

Raspberry Vinaigrette

1/4 cup raspberry vinegar
1/4 cup vegetable oil
3 tablespoons plus 1 teaspoon mayonnaise
1 teaspoon spicy brown mustard
2 teaspoons sugar
Salt and pepper

Melt butter in a heavy skillet. Add pecans and toast over medium heat, stirring for 5 minutes or until brown and crisp.

Toss greens and onion with raspberry vinaigrette. Place salad on 4 serving plates, top each with pecans, blue cheese and crumbled bacon.

Blend all vinaigrette ingredients with whisk and store, tightly covered, in the refrigerator.

Serves 4

Crunchy Salad

1 (5-ounce) bag spring greens
Toasted sliced almonds, as needed
Dried cranberries or tart cherries, as needed
Bite-sized snap peas or green pepper, as needed

Dressing

1/2 cup sugar
1/2 cup salad oil
1/4 cup rice vinegar
2 tablespoons sesame seeds
1/2 teaspoon minced onion (can be dried)
1/4 teaspoon paprika
1/4 teaspoon Worcestershire sauce
Salt and pepper

Mix salad ingredients and dressing ingredients; combine. There will be leftover dressing.

Leslie's Salad

3 (5-ounce) bags mixed salad greens
12 ounces crumbled goat cheese
1 cup dried or fresh berries
1 1/4 cups toasted almond slivers

Dressing

4 cups apple cider reduced to 1/2 cup and cooled
1/4 cup apple cider vinegar
2 tablespoons grated onion
2 tablespoons Dijon mustard
1 tablespoon poppy seeds
1 cup extra virgin olive oil

Combine first 5 ingredients and mix. Whisk in olive oil.

Combine salad ingredients and dressing; toss to blend.

Note: Dressing can be made ahead. Chicken or cold flank steak can be added for a luncheon meal.

Serves 8 to 10

Mark's Everyday Salad

1/4 medium red onion, thinly sliced
4 red radishes, sliced
3/4 cup feta cheese crumbles
Salt and pepper
1/2 head Romaine lettuce
1/2 head red leaf lettuce
1/2 head green leaf lettuce
1/2 cucumber, peeled and sliced

Place onion, radishes and feta in bottom of serving bowl. Add salt and pepper to taste. Top with lettuce and cucumber.

Dressing

1/4 cup extra virgin olive oil
1/4 cup red wine vinegar
1 teaspoon salt
1 teaspoon oregano
1 tablespoon fresh lemon juice
1 garlic clove, peeled and halved

Combine all ingredients. Dress salad to taste.

Zucchini Salad with Red Onion

1	tablespoon red wine vinegar	1/2	small red onion, very thinly sliced
1	tablespoon extra virgin olive oil	4	small zucchini
	Coarse salt and ground pepper		Lettuce leaves

In medium bowl, whisk together vinegar and oil; season with salt and pepper. Stir in onion; let stand 15 minutes.

With a vegetable peeler, slice zucchini into paper-thin ribbons, avoiding seeds. Add to bowl with dressing; season with salt and pepper, if needed. Toss to combine.

Serve on small plate or shallow bowl lined with lettuce leaf; can place tomatoes around edge of plate.

Serves 4

CCVI's Favorite Caesar Salad

2	garlic cloves, minced		Pinch of salt
1	anchovy fillet	1/2	cup extra virgin olive oil
	Freshly ground pepper, to taste	1	small head romaine lettuce
	Juice of 1/2 lemon	1/3	cup ground Parmesan cheese
1	teaspoon white wine vinegar		Plain or Caesar croutons
1/4	teaspoon dry mustard		

Place garlic in a wooden bowl; add anchovy and mash into a paste. Add pepper to mixture. Add lemon juice, vinegar, mustard, salt and olive oil. Mix well with fork and let stand.

Add romaine, Parmesan cheese and croutons. Toss and serve.

Serves 4 to 6

Blue Cheese and Chive Potato Salad

- 8 cups cubed, not peeled, round red potatoes (2 1/2 pounds)
- 1/2 cup diced red onion or scallions
- 1/2 cup diced celery
- 1/4 cup chopped fresh chives
- 3/4 cup nonfat sour cream
- 1/3 cup nonfat buttermilk
- 1/4 teaspoon salt
- 1/2 teaspoon ground black pepper
- 1 1/2 teaspoons cider vinegar
- 1/2 cup (2 ounces) blue cheese, crumbled

Place potatoes in a Dutch oven; cover with water and bring to a boil. Cook 8 minutes or until tender. Drain and place in a large bowl. Add onion, celery and chives; toss gently. Combine sour cream and next 4 ingredients, stir well. Stir in cheese. Pour over potato mixture; toss gently to coat.

Cover and chill.

Serves 8 to 10

Pasta Salad with a Kick

- 4 cups halved vine-ripened cherry tomatoes, or other tomatoes cut into chunks
- 1/3 cup extra virgin olive oil
- 1/2 teaspoon crushed red pepper
- 1/4 teaspoon salt
- 1-2 garlic cloves, lightly crushed
- 1 pound large pasta shapes, such as tri-color fusilli
- 10 fresh basil leaves, finely shredded
- 1 cup freshly grated Pecorino Romano or Asiago cheese
- 1/2 cup toasted pine nuts (optional)

In a large serving bowl, toss tomatoes with oil, red pepper, garlic and salt. Let tomatoes marinate at room temperature for 20 minutes, tossing occasionally.

Bring salted water to a boil; stir in pasta. When water returns to a boil, uncover pot. Cook pasta, stirring occasionally, until al dente (tender but firm) about 12 minutes. Reserve 1/2 cup of pasta cooking water. Drain pasta well.

Stir reserved water and basil into tomatoes. Add pasta and toss to coat. Add cheese and pine nuts, if using. Toss again and serve.

Serves 4 to 6

Cinnamon Honey Fruit Salad

2 tablespoons honey
1 teaspoon cinnamon
Juice of 1 lime
1 tablespoon dark rum (optional)
1 large apple, diced not peeled Fuji or Templeton
1 cup firm red grapes, whole or halved
1 cup firm green grapes, whole or halved
1 cup strawberries or blackberries
Blueberries (optional)
Sprigs of fresh mint (optional)

Whisk honey, cinnamon, lime and rum, if using, in a large bowl. Add fruit (grapes can be halved and strawberries quartered, depending on size). Chill up to 4 hours or serve immediately. Garnish with mint, if desired.

Any combination of color and texture of fruit makes for a great salad.

Serves 6 to 8

Confetti Salad

2 cups orzo pasta
3 tablespoons finely chopped fresh basil
1/4 cup chopped red onion (more to taste)
1/2 cup chopped yellow squash
1/2 cup chopped zucchini
1/4 cup finely chopped raisins
1/4 cup finely chopped toasted almonds
Salt and pepper to taste

Dressing

1 tablespoon sugar
1 tablespoon extra virgin olive oil
2 tablespoons fresh lemon juice
1 tablespoon red wine vinegar
1 tablespoon chopped garlic (optional)

Cook orzo according to package directions. Drain and allow to cool. Mix pasta with basil, onion, squash, zucchini, raisins and almonds. In a small bowl, whisk together sugar, olive oil, lemon, and vinegar. Pour mixture over pasta and season with salt and pepper; chill. If using garlic, mix in after salad is chilled.

Serves 4 to 6

Raspberry Molded Salad

Great replacement for traditional cranberry sauce, especially for holiday dinners.

1 (6-ounce) package raspberry Jell-0
1 1/2 cups boiling water
1 (16-ounce) can whole berry cranberry sauce
1 (15-ounce) can crushed pineapple, drained
1/2 cup chopped walnuts
1 pint raspberry sherbet, softened

Dissolve Jell-O in boiling water. Stir in cranberry sauce, pineapple, and nuts. Whisk in sherbet. Pour into a 9x12-inch pan and refrigerate until set.

Serves 10 to 12

Grilled Corn Salad

8 ears grilled corn, kernels removed
2 sweet onions, halved, thinly sliced
1 pint grape or cherry tomatoes, halved
8 ounces crumbled blue cheese
Fresh basil sprigs

To grill corn prepare a medium-hot grill, remove husks and silks, brush with oil. Grill, turning ears often so they cook evenly, until lightly charred, about 10 minutes.

Mix ingredients and toss with dressing.

Dressing

1/4 cup rice wine vinegar
1/4 cup chopped fresh basil leaves
2 teaspoons honey
1 teaspoon salt, more to taste
1/4 teaspoon pepper, more to taste
1/2 cup extra virgin olive oil

Combine vinegar, basil, honey, salt, pepper and the oil in a blender and blend until smooth. Dressing may be made in advance and refrigerated. Bring to room temperature before using.

Wild Rice and Basil Salad

1	(4-ounce) box wild rice (enough for 2.5 servings)	1	cup loosely packed basil, finely chopped
1	(13 1/2-ounce) can broth (chicken, vegetable or beef)	1	large ripe tomato or 3-4 Roma tomatoes, diced
1	small to medium red onion, diced	4-6	tablespoons extra virgin olive oil

Cook rice in broth (directions on rice package may call for 2 1/2 cups of liquid-disregard). Allow to cool. Mix chopped and diced ingredients, sprinkling with olive oil as needed. Chill covered for several hours or overnight and serve. Flavor improves with chilling. Can easily be made in larger batches.

Serves 4 to 6

Grilled Corn Salad with Black Beans and Rice

2/3	cup short-grain brown rice, cooked al dente, drained and rinsed	1/2	cup spicy hot tomato salsa (optional)
1	(15-ounce) can black beans, drained and rinsed	1/2	cup fresh orange juice
		1/3	cup lime juice
3	large ears corn grilled, slightly charred, kernels cut off	3	tablespoons chopped fresh cilantro
2	medium onions, 3/8-inch slices, grilled and charred	1	tablespoon canola oil
		3/4	teaspoon ground cumin
2	ripe avocados, peeled and diced		Salt and pepper to taste

Mix all together, serve chilled or at room temperature.

Serves 8

Note: Cooked quinoa may be added along with more of the juices and oil. If using the salsa place crushed tortilla chips on top.

Baby Carrot and Vidalia Onion Salad

2 pounds baby carrots, parboiled
1 cup sugar
3/4 cup rice vinegar
1 tablespoon Worcestershire sauce
1 (10 3/4-ounce) can low-sodium tomato soup
Salt and pepper to taste
1 large Vidalia onion, thinly sliced
1 green pepper, thinly sliced

Bring sugar, vinegar, soup and Worcestershire sauce to a boil. Add salt and pepper to taste. Pour over carrots. Add green peppers and onion. Cool and refrigerate. Better after a day or two when flavors have mixed.

Serves 6 to 8

Oriental Rice Salad

2 cups cooked rice, cooled
1/2 pounds fresh bean sprouts
3 stalks celery, sliced
1/2 cup green onion, chopped
1 cup fresh mushrooms, sliced
1/2 cup craisins
1 green pepper, chopped
1/2 bunch parsley or basil, chopped (optional)
1/2 pound fresh spinach, large stems removed
1 cup salted, roasted cashews

Vinaigrette

1/2 cup extra virgin olive oil
1/4 cup low sodium soy sauce
1/2 teaspoon salt
1/4 teaspoon pepper

Mix all salad ingredients except spinach and cashews. Add spinach, cashews and vinaigrette just before serving. Toss until well dressed.

Serves 10 or more

Tip

When using rice in a cold salad, cool and "dry" rice on newspaper for thirty minutes after it is cooked. Newspaper is very clean as it is delivered to you. Never use minute rice for a cold salad.

Crab Salad

Dressing

2 tablespoons red wine vinegar
1 tablespoon Dijon mustard
1 cup olive oil
1/3-1/2 cup orange juice
2 tablespoons orange zest
1/3 cup chopped onion
2 tablespoons chopped fresh dill
1/2 cup chopped cucumber
Salt and pepper to taste

Combine all ingredients.

Salad

3/4 pound cooked crab from crab legs or canned premium
Romaine or Boston lettuce leaves

Cut crab into little pieces. Mix with dressing and serve on lettuce leaves.

Serves 4 to 6

Wild Rice Salad

Dressing

1/2 cup canola oil
1/4 cup white vinegar
1/4 cup grated Parmesan
1 1/2 teaspoons sugar
1/2 teaspoon salt
1/2 teaspoon celery seed
1/4 teaspoon black pepper
1/4 teaspoon dry mustard
1/8 teaspoon paprika
1 clove garlic, minced

Combine all ingredients and shake to mix.

Salad

1 (5-6 ounce) bag mixed greens
1 cup cooked long grain and wild rice
1 cup frozen peas, thawed
1 (7.5-ounce) jar marinated artichokes, chopped
2 cups cooked shredded chicken (optional)
1/3 cup red bell pepper, chopped
3 green onions, chopped
1 cup grape tomatoes, halved
1/4 cup slivered almonds
1/4 cup fresh basil leaves, torn (optional)

Combine ingredients and dress.

Serves 8 as a side, 4 as a main course

Cuban Chicken Salad

Anne Liston, Head Chef, Phillip R, Shriver Center, Miami of Ohio University

2 (10-ounce) packages chopped romaine lettuce, more or less as needed
2 pounds corn relish (recipe follows)
1/2 cup sun-dried tomato bits packed in oil
1 (15-ounce) can black beans, drained and rinsed
2 pounds packaged chicken fajita meat
12 ounces cheese queso fresco (Mexican cheese), coarse shred
2 ounces sliced ripe olives
6 ounces diced red peppers
6 ounces diced yellow peppers
2 ounces raw pumpkin seeds, toasted
8 (2-ounce) portions of Ranch dressing (recipe follows)

To assemble 8 individual chilled plates: place 2 to 3 ounces romaine on plate, center 4 ounces of corn relish on romaine. Scatter over plate 1 tablespoon sun-dried tomatoes, 2 ounces black beans followed by 4 ounces of chicken. Top corn relish with 1.5 ounces cheese and black olives. Scatter pepper strips and pumpkin seeds over all. Serve with dressing on side.

Corn relish

1 (16-ounce) bag frozen corn, totally defrosted
1 (6-ounce) can diced green chiles
1/2 cup diced yellow pepper
1/2 cup diced red pepper
1/2 cup diced green pepper
1 medium tomato, diced
1 jalapeno pepper, finely diced
1 small red onion, finely diced
2 tablespoons chopped cilantro
1 clove garlic, minced
1 teaspoon salt
2 teaspoons chopped chives
1/2 teaspoon chili powder
2 tablespoons lime juice
2 teaspoons honey
2 teaspoons white vinegar

Combine corn, chiles, peppers, tomato and onion. Mix spices and herbs with lime, honey and vinegar. Pour dressing over vegetables and mix gently.

Dressing

Combine 10 ounces of bottled peppercorn ranch dressing (Marzetti or Kraft suggested) and 5 ounces guacamole. Serve on side.

Crispy Chinese Chicken Salad

Salad

- 2 1/2 pounds chicken breasts, (bone in and skin on)
- Kosher salt
- Fresh ground black pepper
- 8 Wonton wrappers
- Pam
- 1/2 cup snow peas, trimmed and diagonally cut into thirds
- 3 large scallions, thinly sliced on diagonal (white and green)
- 3 1/2 cups sliced Napa cabbage, (1/2-inch strips)
- 1 1/2 -2 cups sliced heart of Romaine lettuce (1/2-inch strips)
- 1 tablespoon white sesame seeds, slightly toasted
- 2/3 cup sliced almonds, toasted

Preheat oven to 425 degrees. Season chicken breasts and roast 40-45 minutes, cool, remove bones and skin, shred meat. Set aside.

Reduce oven to 375 degrees. Line baking sheet with foil; place 1/2-inch strips of wontons on sheet, spray lightly with Pam and sprinkle with salt. Push strips into "wavy" shapes before baking 7-9 minutes. Set aside.

Blanche snow peas in salted water 20 seconds (bright green and crisp). Immediately plunge into ice water; dry.

Dressing

- 1/4 cup rice vinegar
- 1 1/2 tablespoons Tamari or soy sauce
- 1 tablespoon Sweet Asian Chile Sauce
- 2 medium cloves garlic, finely chopped
- 2 teaspoons minced fresh ginger
- 1/2 teaspoon kosher salt
- 1/4 teaspoon freshly ground black pepper
- 1/4 cup peanut oil
- 1 tablespoon sesame oil
- 1/2 teaspoon Hot Asian Chile Sauce, optional

Combine vinegar, Tamari, chile sauce, garlic, ginger, salt and pepper. Gradually whisk in oils. Let blend for at least 1 hour; strain.

Combine chicken and scallions with 1/4 cup dressing; toss with greens and peas. Add sesame seeds and almonds, toss with dressing to coat. Place on large serving platter or individual plates and garnish with wonton strips

Serves 4 to 6

Chinese Chicken Salad

Serve with toasted French bread for a great luncheon.

1/2 head iceberg lettuce, or other "stiff" greens
1/2 cup cilantro
1 (8-ounce) can sliced water chestnuts
4 cups cooked chicken breast, shredded
8 green onions, sliced
4 tablespoons sesame seeds, toasted
1 (4-ounce) package slivered almonds, toasted
1 (5-ounce) can Chinese noodles

Dressing

4 tablespoons sugar
2 teaspoons salt
1/4 teaspoon pepper
4 tablespoons rice vinegar
1/4 cup salad oil
1/4 cup sesame oil

Mix all salad ingredients in large bowl except Chinese noodles. Whisk all dressing ingredients together. Dress salad before serving and sprinkle noodles on top.

Serves 4 to 6

CCVI Staff's Favorite Hot Chicken Salad

2+ cups diced cooked chicken
1 (10.75-ounce) can cream of chicken soup
3/4 cup Hellman's mayonnaise
1 cup chopped celery
1/2 cup finely chopped onion
1 cup cooked rice
1 (8-ounce) can sliced water chestnuts, drained
1 tablespoon lemon juice
Salt to taste
1 cup buttered corn flakes
1 cup slivered almonds

Preheat oven to 350 degrees. Mix all ingredients except corn flakes and almonds. Pour into greased 9 x 13-inch pan. Top with corn flakes and almonds and bake 1/2 hour or until browned and bubbly.

Chicken Salad with Pasta and Spinach

1 (16-ounce) package of gnocchi pasta (not potato) or medium shell pasta
5 cups shredded or cubed cooked chicken
3/4 cup thinly sliced celery
3/4 cup chopped red onion
1 1/4 cup mayonnaise
1 1/4 cups bottled Briannas Poppy Seed salad dressing
1 1/2 teaspoons salt
1/4 teaspoon pepper
1 (5-ounce) package baby spinach, stems removed
1 cup coarsely chopped toasted pecans
1 (5-ounce) package dried red cherries
Curly leaf red lettuce or any choice of lettuce for presenting the salad.

Cook pasta according to directions on package. Rinse, drain and pat dry. In a large bowl, combine chicken, celery and onion. Combine mayonnaise with salad dressing and salt and pepper. Fold 1 3/4 cups dressing into pasta and add to chicken mixture. Cover tightly and refrigerate up to one day. Before serving, add remaining dressing, spinach, pecans and cherries and toss well.

Note: For a different flavor try using Briannas Blush Wine Vinaigrette.

Serves 12 to 14

South of the Border

1 (15-ounce) can black beans, rinsed and drained
1 (15-ounce) can garbanzo beans, rinsed and drained
1 orange, peeled, quartered and sliced
1 small yellow bell pepper, diced
1/3 cup finely chopped cilantro
1/2 cup bottled fruit vinaigrette
3/4 teaspoon chili powder
6 red radishes, thinly sliced
1 ripe avocado, peeled and cubed

In large bowl combine beans, orange, bell pepper, cilantro, vinaigrette and chili powder; toss to mix and coat. Before serving add radishes and avocado.

Serves 8

Side Dishes

Menu Ideas

Sun-Dried Tomato Spread	15
Rotisserie Chicken and Rice	111
Roasted Asparagus with Lemon	78
Watermelon Salsa	94
Gooey Butter Coconut Bars	130
Lemon Crisps	147

Side Dishes

Baked Sliced Apples

4 Jonathan apples, peeled, cored and sliced
Juice of 1 lemon
1/4 cup brown sugar
1/2 cup butter, cubed
Cinnamon
Freshly grated nutmeg

Preheat oven to 350 degrees. Mix apples with lemon juice and stir in brown sugar. Sprinkle butter over all. Shake cinnamon over and add nutmeg. Bake in 6 x 10-inch or smaller dish for 20 minutes, until apples are tender.

Serves 4

Note: Cooking apples other than Jonathan may be substituted, but they should be of a red hue; leave a few peels in place for coloring. Remove peels before serving.

Roasted Asparagus with Lemon

1 pound asparagus
3 tablespoons extra virgin olive oil
2 garlic cloves, minced
Zest of 1 lemon
Salt and freshly ground black pepper
1 lemon, cut in wedges

Preheat broiler. Snap off tough ends of asparagus and arrange spears on a baking sheet. Whisk together olive oil, garlic and zest and pour over asparagus; toss to coat well and season with salt and pepper. Arrange lemon wedges around asparagus. Broil 6 inches from heat (keep oven door partially open if using an electric oven) 5-10 minutes until tender and golden. Transfer to serving platter and drizzle with pan juices.

Serves 4

Note: Choose spears with bright green stalks and purple tips.

St. Croix Cabbage

1 head red cabbage
1 (5.5-ounce) can apple juice
1 apple

Wash and core cabbage and remove outside leaves. Slice into 2-inch wedges. Core apple and dice into 1-inch cubes. Fry apple in bacon grease or canola oil until soft. Add juice and cabbage, cover and cook until cabbage is soft.

Note: Bacon grease gives this the best flavor.

Honey-Glazed Baby Carrots

1 pound fresh baby carrots
1/4 cup water
1/4 cup honey
2 tablespoons butter
2 tablespoons dark brown sugar, packed
1 tablespoon white wine vinegar
1/2 teaspoon salt
1/8 teaspoon allspice

In a large skillet combine all ingredients over medium-high heat. Bring to a boil. Reduce heat to medium; cover and simmer approximately 20 minutes or until carrots are almost tender. Cook, uncovered, approximately 10 minutes longer, or until carrots are tender and liquid is reduced to a glaze.

Serves 6

Note: Carrots may be roasted until tender for more crispness. Glaze can be prepared on stove top.

Carrot and Parsnip Fries

Kids and kids at heart will love these.

1 pound carrots
best straight from a farmer's market
1 pound parsnips
2 tablespoons olive oil
Sea salt

Preheat oven to 425 degrees. Clean and trim vegetables; cut into halves or quarters. Toss with oil and place cut side down in a single layer on a baking sheet; generously sprinkle with salt. Bake 15-20 minutes or until golden.

Chickpea Salad

- 2 tablespoons olive oil
- 1 pound carrots, peeled and sliced into 1/4 inch rounds
- 1/2 cup chicken or vegetable stock
- 1 (15-ounce) can chickpeas, drained and rinsed
- 2 teaspoons ground cumin
- 1 teaspoon paprika
- 1 tablespoon lemon juice
- 1 small red onion, thinly sliced (1 cup)
- 8 cups watercress, washed and dried

In large sauté pan heat 1 tablespoon oil. Add carrots and cook over medium-high heat 5 minutes. Reduce heat to low, add 1/4 cup stock, cover and cook until liquid is absorbed, about 7 minutes. Add chickpeas, cumin and paprika and cook over medium heat, stirring, 2 minutes. Add remaining stock and cook, uncovered, until liquid is absorbed, 2-3 minutes. Remove from heat and add lemon juice, onion, watercress and remaining olive oil. Toss well and serve warm or at room temperature.

Serves 8

Scout Corn

A crowd pleaser, served yearly at a Boy Scout banquet.

- 40 ounces frozen corn
- 2 (8-ounce) packages cream cheese, quartered
- 1 cup butter, quartered
- 10 tablespoons water
- 6 tablespoons sugar

Mix together all ingredients. Place in crock pot and set on high 4 hours or low 6; stir periodically.

Serves 25

Green Bean Casserole with Fried Leeks

2 tablespoons butter
2 (8-ounce) packages sliced fresh mushrooms
1 teaspoon dried thyme
2 shallots, finely chopped
1/2 cup Madeira wine
1 cup heavy cream
1 1/4 pounds fresh green beans, trimmed
Vegetable or peanut oil
2 large leeks, cleaned and thinly sliced crosswise (white and light green only)
Sea salt

Preheat oven to 400 degrees. Melt butter in large heavy skillet over medium-high heat. Add mushrooms and thyme; sauté 5 minutes. Add shallots; sauté 3 minutes or until tender. Add Madeira and cook over medium-high heat 3 minutes or until liquid evaporates. Add cream and cook 2-5 minutes or until slightly thickened. Remove from heat.

Cook beans in small amount of water 5 minutes or until just crisp-tender; drain. Add beans to mushroom mixture and toss gently. Place in a greased 2-quart baking dish. Cover to keep warm.

Pour oil to depth of 2 inches into a 3-quart saucepan; heat to 350 degrees. Fry leeks in 3 batches, 40 seconds or until golden. Remove leeks with strainer, drain on paper towels. Sprinkle with salt. Sprinkle leeks over warm bean mixture. Bake, uncovered, 5 minutes or until casserole is heated through.

Serves 6

Sichuan Green Beans

2 cups green beans (young and tender)
1 tablespoon minced fresh ginger
1 teaspoon minced garlic
4 scallions, thinly sliced
1 tablespoon canola oil

Sauce

2 tablespoons Chinese bean paste
2 tablespoons soy sauce
1/2 teaspoon hot chili sauce (sold as sambal oelek)
1/4 cup water

Mix together ingredients for sauce. Heat oil in wok over high heat. When very hot add green beans, ginger, garlic and scallions. Sauté until beans begin to brown on edges but remain crisp in center. Quickly add sauce and cook until sauce has reduced by half, about 1 minute. Serve hot.

Serves 4

Note: Sambal oelek is available in Asian section of grocery stores.

Chile Potatoes

Spicy and great for a barbeque.

- 4 large Russet potatoes, peeled and thinly sliced
- 1 tablespoon tomato paste
- 2 tablespoons garlic puree
- 1 tablespoon chipotle pepper in adobo puree
- 1 tablespoon smoked paprika
- 1 cup whole milk
- 1 cup heavy cream
- 1 cup shredded sharp Cheddar cheese
- Salt and pepper

Preheat oven to 350 degrees. Combine all ingredients in a large bowl and season with salt and pepper to taste. Place mixture in baking dish and bake until potatoes are tender, approximately 30 minutes.

Serves 6

Braised Leeks in Mustard Sauce

- 4 leeks, cleaned, halved, cut 8 inches long, green ends scored
- 1 bunch scallions, bulb and green ends chopped and set aside
- 2 tablespoons butter
- 1/4 cup dry vermouth
- 1 cup chicken stock

Sauce

- 3 tablespoons Coleman's dry mustard
- 3 tablespoons cider vinegar
- 2 eggs, beaten
- 3/4 cup heavy cream
- 2 tablespoons sugar
- 1/4 teaspoon salt
- 1 1/2-2 tablespoons butter
- 2 tablespoons poaching liquid from leeks

Leeks: In a large skillet sauté bulb ends of scallions in butter until limp; do not brown. Add vermouth, cook briefly and add chicken stock. Arrange leeks in skillet, sprinkle with green ends of scallions. Reduce heat, cover pan, cook 8-10 minutes. Drain on paper towel. Reserve liquids.

Sauce: Combine mustard, sugar, salt and vinegar in top of a double boiler; beat with whisk to remove all lumps. Add eggs and butter, cook and beat over low heat until thick. Slowly beat in cream. If made ahead, refrigerate. Before serving reheat slowly and add leek liquid; do not let temperature go above 150 degrees. Sauce should be the consistency of a medium white sauce.

Serves 4

Creamed Leeks

1 leek per person
Olive oil
Salt and pepper
Heavy cream or half-and-half

Cut off hard and woody green ends of leeks. Cut leeks lengthwise to clean. Cut off root ends. Slice into half moon shapes about 1/2-inch thick. Sauté in olive oil about 20 minutes until tender. Add salt and pepper as leeks start to soften. Five minutes before serving add a few tablespoons cream or half-and-half and stir to thicken.

Potatoes and Squash

1 1 1/4 -1 1/2 pound butternut squash, peeled, seeded and cubed (4 cups)
2 cups peeled, cubed sweet and/ or white potatoes
1/2 cup chopped red bell pepper
1 cup water
1/2 cup thin wedges yellow onion
2 cloves garlic, minced
1/4 cup olive oil
1 tablespoon brown sugar, packed
1 teaspoon snipped fresh thyme
1 teaspoon snipped fresh basil
1/2 teaspoon salt
1/4 teaspoon crushed red pepper
1/4 teaspoon ground black pepper

In skillet combine squash, potatoes and water, bring to a boil and reduce heat; simmer, covered 8-10 minutes or until vegetables are tender. Drain and set aside. In same skillet cook red pepper, onion and garlic in hot olive oil over medium heat until onion is tender.

Stir in brown sugar, remove from heat and stir in thyme, basil, salt and peppers. Combine mixtures.

Serves 8 to 10

Potatoes Boursin

- 1 (7-ounce) block Boursin cheese with herbs, cubed
- 1 cup half-and-half
- 3 pounds new potatoes, unpeeled and thinly sliced
- Salt and pepper
- 1 tablespoon fresh parsley, divided
- 1 teaspoon butter

Preheat oven to 400 degrees. Cook cheese and half-and-half in saucepan over medium heat, stirring constantly, until lumps disappear. Arrange half of potato slices in lightly greased 9 x 13-inch baking dish, overlapping edges. Sprinkle with salt and pepper and 1/2 of the parsley. Pour 1/2 of the cheese mixture over potato slices, repeating layer once. Dot top with butter. Bake 1 hour or until golden and bubbly.

Spinach Timbales

- 2 cups spinach, blanched and chopped or 2 (10-ounce) packages whole frozen, well-drained and chopped
- 1 small yellow onion, chopped
- 5 tablespoons butter
- Salt and freshly ground pepper
- 1/8 teaspoon nutmeg
- 1 1/2 cups milk or half-and-half
- 4 eggs
- 1/2 cup grated Swiss or Gruyère cheese

Preheat oven to 325 degrees. Melt 2 tablespoons butter in a saucepan and add onion; cook until translucent, not brown. Add spinach and cook until moisture is evaporated, then add 3 tablespoons butter and stir until butter is absorbed by the spinach. Season with salt, pepper and nutmeg. Add milk and cook until slightly warmed. Lightly beat eggs and mix in; add cheese and stir until thoroughly combined.

Butter 4 individual molds or a 6-cup mold; pour mixture into mold(s). Place in a pan and add water halfway up the sides of the molds. Bake 20 minutes for individual molds or 30-40 for larger. Molds are done when a toothpick inserted in center comes out clean. Unmold and serve.

Serves 4

Acorn Squash

1 acorn squash
1 tablespoon butter
1-2 tablespoons brown sugar

Preheat oven to 350 degrees. Cut squash in half; scoop out seeds. Place pat of butter and 1-2 tablespoons sugar in hollow of squash. Place cut side up in roasting pan with sides. Add about 1 inch of water. Bake1 hour.

Summer Vegetable Tian

3/4 cup olive oil plus more for pan
1/2 large yellow onion, diced
1 red bell pepper, seeded, cut into 1/8-inch strips
5 garlic cloves, minced
Salt and freshly ground pepper
3 small zucchini, cut into 1/8-inch rounds
2 small yellow squash, cut into 1/8-rounds
1 teaspoon finely chopped fresh rosemary or 1/2 teaspoon dried
1 teaspoon finely chopped fresh thyme or 1/2 teaspoon dried
1 pound plum tomatoes, cut into 1/8-inch rounds
1/2 cup grated Parmigiano-Reggiano cheese
1/2 cup fine dried bread crumbs

Preheat oven to 350 degrees. Lightly coat a 2-quart baking dish with oil.

In a frying pan over medium heat, warm 5 tablespoons olive oil. Add onion and sauté until translucent, 5-10 minutes. Add bell pepper and garlic, season with salt and pepper. Cook, stirring occasionally, until softened, 5-10 minutes. Transfer mixture to the prepared dish and spread evenly. Set aside.

In a bowl combine zucchini, yellow squash, 5 tablespoons oil, rosemary, thyme, salt and pepper and stir to evenly coat. Arrange zucchini, squash and tomato slices on onion-pepper mixture, overlapping the rows. Drizzle with remaining 2 tablespoons oil and bake 30 minutes.

Mix together cheese and bread crumbs. Remove baking dish from oven and sprinkle crumb mixture on top. Bake 15 more minutes.

Broil until cheese is golden brown, 5-8 minutes. Let stand 10 minutes before serving.

Serves 6

Spaghetti Squash Piperade

1 medium squash, cut lengthwise in half, seeds removed
3 tablespoons butter

Piperade

1 clove garlic, minced
1 medium onion, chopped
3 tablespoons olive oil
1 large green bell pepper
1 large red bell pepper
2 banana peppers
2 (15-ounce) cans Italian tomatoes, drained and chopped or 4 fresh, peeled and seeded
Minced parsley
1/3 cup black olives, chopped
2 teaspoons tomato paste
1/2 teaspoon crushed red pepper
1/8 teaspoon sugar
1/4 teaspoon salt
Ground black pepper

Piperade: Seed peppers, cut into bite-size pieces. Sauté garlic and onion in oil until limp. Add peppers, sauté slightly; add tomatoes. Lower heat, cover, cook 8-10 minutes until peppers are crisp. Stir in tomato paste and seasonings. Add chopped parsley and olives. Serve hot or cold. May be made ahead and frozen.

Squash: Preheat oven to 375 degrees. Place squash cut side down in pan of hot water with 2 teaspoons salt. Cover with foil and bake 30 minutes. Remove, drain on towel. Remove pulp with fork and toss with 3 tablespoons butter. Place on platter and top with piperade.

Serves 6 to 8

Sophie's Ratatouille

1 yellow onion
1 green bell pepper
1 red bell pepper
2 globe eggplants
2 zucchini
3 ripe tomatoes
Salt and pepper
Thyme
Olive Oil

Cut onion in half and then into thin slices. Cook in olive oil until translucent. Cube all other vegetables. Cook them individually (except tomatoes) in a sauté pan for approximately 15 minutes per vegetable. Once cooked, combine all vegetables, add cubed tomatoes, and season with salt and pepper. Adjust flavor with thyme and simmer over low heat for 30 minutes.

Serves 4 to 6

Note: Leftovers may be reheated and served over polenta mixed with Parmesan cheese.

Tahitian Rice

1/2 cup butter
2 cups rice
3 1/2 cups boiling water
4 tablespoons chicken bouillon
4 tablespoons soy sauce
1/2 cup slivered almonds
5 green onions, tops only

Melt butter, stir in rice. Dissolve bouillon in water and add to rice. Cook over low heat 20 minutes or until all liquid is absorbed. Remove from heat and add almonds, soy sauce and onion tops. Let stand 15 minutes. Can be prepared ahead and reheated.

Serves 8

Goat Cheese Gnocchi

Ted Habiger, Room 39
1719 West 39th Street, Kansas City, MO

Gnocchi

2 pounds goat cheese hung in cheesecloth overnight then squeezed
2 egg yolks
1/2 cup grated Pecorino Romano
1 tablespoon salt
1/2-1 cup flour

Combine cheeses, yolks and salt in a stainless steel bowl. Mix well with your hands. Push mixture into bottom of bowl and indent with finger tips. Sprinkle 1/2 cup flour over dough and knead mixture with quarter turns. Continue kneading for several minutes, test a small amount by dropping a small gnocchi into boiling water. If it falls apart repeat flour step. When dough is complete, put in a piping bag and pipe out long tubes. Cut into 1-inch pieces and hand roll then freeze. This gnocchi is fragile and best cooked frozen. Boil as pasta; when gnocchi is ready it will float.

Sauce

4 yellow onions, thinly sliced
4 shallots, thinly sliced
8 cloves of garlic, thinly sliced
Parsley, tarragon or basil, chopped
Bay leaves
2 lemons, juice and zest
2 cups white wine
4 quarts heavy cream
Kosher salt and freshly ground black pepper

In a medium Dutch oven slowly cook onions, shallots, garlic, parsley and bay leaves with a little oil several minutes until soft but very little color. Add lemon zest and juice. Add white wine and cook slowly over medium heat until almost dry. Add cream and cook over medium heat until sauce coats the back of a spoon. Strain through a chinois and adjust seasoning.

Makes about 100 gnocchi; keep frozen, use as needed.

Note: Sauce ingredients can be easily halved or quartered for a smaller quantity.

Wild Rice and Chana Dal Pilaf

Ted Habiger, Room 39
1719 West 39th Street, Kansas City, MO

1 medium yellow onion, diced
2 bay leaves
1 cup long grain wild rice, rinsed
1/2 cup chana dal (yellow split peas)

In a small saucepan bring 2 cups water to boil. Add rice, 1/2 of onion and bay leaf and reduce to a simmer, stirring occasionally. Add more water if too much is absorbed by rice and cook for 20-30 minutes. Test rice for doneness by tasting a grain. Strain out excess water and set rice aside to cool.

In a small saucepan bring 1 cup water to a boil. Add the chana dal, other 1/2 of onion and bay leaf. Reduce heat and cook uncovered until dal is cooked through, about 15 minutes. Strain out excess water and set dal aside to cool.

Finishing

2 tablespoons butter
1 medium yellow onion, chopped
1/2 cup pecans
1 cup assorted mushrooms (shiitakes, portobellas, criminis or oyster)
Salt and pepper

In a large skillet melt butter and add chopped onion. Sauté until onion is translucent and add the mushrooms. Cook for 5-7 minutes, trying to brown mushrooms just slightly. Add pecans, rice and chana dal to pan. Add a small amount of water to help steam everything. Mix well, season with salt and pepper and serve.

Serves 6

Note: 1/2 teaspoon iodized salt = 1 teaspoon kosher salt.

Summertime Wheat Berry Salad

An unusual and tasty side dish for a grilling party.

1 cup wheat berries
3 cups water
1/2 teaspoon salt
1 red bell pepper, chopped
3 green onions, chopped
2 Roma tomatoes, seeded and chopped
1 small cucumber, unpeeled and diced
3/4 cup edamame
1/3 cup chopped fresh Italian parsley
2 tablespoons fresh minced tarragon

Dressing

2 tablespoons lemon juice
2 tablespoons sherry vinegar
1 tablespoon Dijon mustard
1/2 cup plain nonfat yogurt
1 tablespoon olive oil
Salt and pepper

In a medium saucepan bring water and wheat to a boil. Add salt; cover and simmer 1 hour or until wheat is cooked through. (Berries will remain chewy). Drain and place in large bowl. Add red pepper, onions, tomatoes, cucumber, edamame, parsley and tarragon. Toss to combine.

Dressing: Combine lemon juice, vinegar, mustard and yogurt; blend well. Whisk in oil until blended. Season to taste with salt and pepper. Pour over salad and toss to combine.

Serves 8

Provençal Tomatoes

4 ripe tomatoes
Sea salt and pepper
Herbes de Provence
4 cloves garlic
Fresh bread crumbs
Olive oil

Preheat oven to 350 degrees. Core and cut each tomato in half. Season with salt, pepper and herbes de Provence. Slice garlic clove thinly and distribute over tomato halves. Sprinkle with fresh bread crumbs and drizzle with olive oil. Bake on cookie sheet for 30 minutes.

Herb and Goat Cheese Souffle

1/4 cup extra virgin olive oil
5 tablespoons flour
1 large garlic clove, minced
1 1/2 cups whole milk
1/4 cup dry white wine
6 large egg yolks
1 teaspoon salt
Pepper to taste
8 large egg whites
1 tablespoon minced fresh basil
1 tablespoon minced fresh thyme
1 teaspoon minced fresh rosemary
1 cup crumbled and chilled soft fresh goat cheese
1/2 cup grated Gruyère, packed (about 2-ounces)

Preheat oven to 400 degrees. Position rack in center of oven. Generously butter soufflé dish or ramekins. If using ramekins place in rimmed baking pan.

Heat oil in heavy large saucepan, add flour and garlic; cook without browning, whisking constantly, until mixture begins to bubble, about 1 minute. Gradually whisk in milk and wine. Cook until smooth and thick and beginning to boil, whisking constantly, about 2 minutes. Remove from heat.

Mix egg yolks, salt and pepper in small bowl. Add yolk mixture all at once to sauce and whisk quickly to blend. Mix in basil, thyme and rosemary. Fold in cheeses; they do not need to melt. Using an electric mixer beat egg whites until stiff but not dry. Fold 1/4 of the whites into lukewarm soufflé base to lighten. Fold in remaining whites. Transfer soufflé mixture to prepared dish and sprinkle with pepper.

Place soufflé in oven. Reduce heat to 375 degrees. Bake until puffed, golden and partially set in center, about 35 minutes for large or 25 minutes for small. Serve immediately.

Serves 4 to 6

Mango Salsa

2 large ripe mangoes, peeled, cubed
1 ripe avocado; halved, pitted, peeled and diced
1/2 fresh jalapeno pepper, seeded, minced
1/3 cup diced red onion
1 teaspoon grated lime zest
3 tablespoons fresh lime juice
1/4 cup fresh orange juice
1/4 cup chopped fresh cilantro
1 tablespoon olive oil
Salt and pepper

Mix all ingredients and season with salt and pepper.

Cheese Pudding

1/2 pound butter, melted
1 1/2 pounds grated sharp cheese (not packaged shredded)
20 slices bread, crust trimmed and cubed
4 cups whole milk
4 large eggs, separated
1 teaspoon salt
1 teaspoon red pepper
1 teaspoon dry mustard

Combine butter, cheese, bread and egg yolks. Mix milk and seasonings and pour over bread. Beat egg whites until firm but not dry and fold into bread mixture. Hold mixture in a bowl in refrigerator overnight or at least 12 hours. Preheat oven to 350 degrees. Pour into prepared 9 x 13-inch baking dish and bake 80 minutes or until well browned and crusty around the edges.

Serves 10 to 12

Note: Cracker Barrel Sharp Cheddar Cheese and Sara Lee White Bread with Whole Grain are suggested.

Strawberry Tomato Salsa

1 pint fresh strawberries, chopped
4 plum or Roma tomatoes, chopped
1 small red onion, finely chopped
1-2 medium jalapeno peppers, seeded and minced
2 garlic cloves, minced
1 tablespoon olive oil
Juice of 1 lime
Cilantro, chopped (optional)

Combine all ingredients, cover and chill at least 2 hours.

Note: Serve over grilled chicken or pork as well as with chips.

Cranberry Pear Chutney

4 cups fresh cranberries
1 1/2 cups brown sugar, packed
2 cups water
2 Bosc or Asian pears, peeled and cut into small dice (2 cups)
1 jalapeno, seeded and minced
1 cup golden raisins
2 tablespoons lime juice

In a large saucepan heat cranberries, sugar and 2 cups of water over medium-high heat to boiling. Simmer, stirring occasionally, until cranberries start to pop and release juices, about 10 minutes. Add pears, jalapeno, raisins and lime juice; simmer 5 minutes. Remove from heat, cool, cover and refrigerate up to 2 days.

Serves 8

Note: Perfect for roast turkey.

Fruit Salsa with Cinnamon Crisps

1 pint fresh strawberries, chopped
1 (8-ounce) can crushed pineapple, drained
1 Red Delicious apple, chopped
1 kiwifruit, peeled and chopped
1/4 cup fresh lemon juice
1/4 cup sugar
1/4 teaspoon nutmeg
1 1/4 teaspoons cinnamon, divided
4 (7 1/2-inch) flour tortillas
Vegetable cooking spray
2 tablespoons sugar

Combine first 4 ingredients. Stir together lemon juice, sugar, nutmeg and 1/2 teaspoon cinnamon; toss with fruit. Chill.

Preheat oven to 350 degrees. Cut each tortilla into eights. Arrange pieces on baking sheets. Lightly coat with cooking spray. Combine remaining 3/4 teaspoon cinnamon and sugar. Sprinkle over chips. Bake 6-8 minutes or until lightly browned.

Serve with fruit salsa.

Serves 4

Watermelon Salsa

2 cups watermelon, seeded and cubed
1 cup chopped pineapple
1 cup mango, peeled and cubed
Juice from 4 limes
1 cup scallions, chopped
1/2 cup chopped cilantro
Salt and pepper

Combine all ingredients. Refrigerate before serving.

Serves 8 to 12

Apple Mango Chutney

1 pound apples, peeled, seeded, finely chopped
1 1/2 cups white wine vinegar
3/4 cup brown sugar
1 teaspoon green chiles, finely chopped
1 cup raisins, red or white
2 tablespoons currants
2 cloves garlic, crushed
Zest of 1 lemon
1 cup mango chunks
1/2 teaspoon salt
1 tablespoon mustard seed
1 tablespoon ginger

Bring apples and vinegar to a boil and cook 5 minutes. Add sugar, chiles, raisins, currants, garlic and zest. Simmer 15 minutes. Add mangoes and seasoning. Cook 30 minutes.

Note: Pour into sterilized small jelly jars and place in a water bath to make great hostess gifts.

Entrees

Menu Ideas

Candlelight Smoked Salmon Cheesecake . . .	6
Beef Tenderloin with Burgundy Wine Sauce. . .	97
or Burgundy Tenderloin Fillets.	98
or Killer Filet of Beef.	100
Putch's 210 Salad . . . . (*Then and Now*)	117
or Tangy Bayside Salad	63
Wild Rice and Chana Dal Pilaf.	89
Green Bean Casserole with Fried Leeks	81
Chocolate Orange Tart	136
or Poached Pears in Zabaglione Sauce	138

Entrees

Beef Tenderloin with Burgundy Wine Sauce

1 4-pound beef tenderloin, room temperature
Onion salt
Garlic salt
Celery salt
Seasoned salt
Pepper

Preheat oven to 300 degrees. Liberally coat meat with salts and pepper. Place under preheated broiler 3 minutes per side (do not overdo). Set aside to cool to room temperature.

Place meat on an ovenproof platter or pan, saving original pan and juices for sauce, bake 1 hour. Let rest before slicing.

Sauce

2 1/2 tablespoons finely minced onion or shallot
4 tablespoons butter, divided
1 1/4 cups Burgundy wine plus 5 tablespoons
2 1/2 teaspoons flour

Sauté onions or shallots in 1 1/2 tablespoons butter and pan juices 1 minute; add 1 1/4 cups wine and cook until reduced to 1/2 of original volume. Stir in flour and 2 1/2 teaspoons butter and mix to a smooth paste. When butter is melted, add 5 tablespoons wine. Spoon sauce over meat portions and serve.

Serves 8 to 10

Tip

Don't throw away leftover wine. Freeze into ice cubes for future use in casseroles and sauces.

Burgundy Tenderloin Fillets

2 tablespoons butter
6 fillet mignon steaks, 1 1/4-inch thick
1/2 cup chopped mushrooms
1/2 cup chopped onions
4 teaspoons cornstarch
1/2 cup cold water
1 cup Burgundy wine
2 tablespoons parsley, chopped
1 teaspoon salt
Dash of pepper
6 large mushrooms

Preheat oven to 500 degrees. Quickly brown both sides of fillets in butter, reserving butter. Place each fillet on separate 8-inch squares of heavy-duty foil. Sauté mushrooms and onions in reserved butter. Blend cornstarch with cold water and add to mushroom mixture along with wine. Add parsley, salt and pepper and cook until slightly thickened. Spoon 2 tablespoons of mixture over each fillet, reserving remainder for additional serving sauce. Place a mushroom cap on top of each fillet and bring corners of foil together; do not make airtight. Bake 12 minutes for rare, 15 minutes for medium and 18 minutes for well done. Reheat remaining sauce for gravy.

Note: Allow 10 minutes extra cooking time if fillets have been refrigerated prior to cooking.

Serves 6

Laura's Brisket

1 8-10 pound brisket
2-3 tablespoons onion powder
2-3 tablespoons garlic salt
1/2 cup Worcestershire sauce
2 (4-ounce) bottles of Figaro Hickory Flavored liquid smoke

Mix dry ingredients in a small bowl. Rub generously on both sides of meat. Place meat, fat side up, in a roasting pan. Pour Worcestershire sauce and liquid smoke over meat. Cover with foil and refrigerate overnight.

Preheat oven to 275 degrees. Bake 6-8 hours or until meat is fork tender. Cool with foil tented. Remove excess fat and carve meat. Cut against grain into slices. Place slices back into pan of drippings and refrigerate until ready to eat. If more "gravy" is desired, add small amount of water or broth. Before serving allow to come to room temperature, warm in a 275 degree oven for 30-45 minutes.

Note: This can be taken when you need to make something for a condolence call.

Brisket

1 6-7 1/2 pound brisket
2 tablespoons Worcestershire sauce
1/3 cup soy sauce
1 box (2-ounce) French onion soup
1/2 can beer or 7-up

Preheat oven to 275 degrees. Place enough foil to surround brisket in 9x13-inch pan. Pour other ingredients over brisket and seal foil. Bake 45 to 60 minutes per pound. Cool before slicing meat. Reheat in remaining liquid and serve with a small amount of liquid.

Serves 10 to 20, depending on size of Brisket.

Beef Kabobs

3 pounds sirloin, cut in 1-inch cubes

Marinade
1 (1-ounce) envelope dry onion soup mix
1/4 cup sugar
1 cup catsup
1/2 cup vinegar
1/2 cup salad oil
2 tablespoons prepared mustard
Dash of bottled hot pepper sauce

Possible vegetables
Onion
Sweet red pepper
Green pepper
Mushrooms
Cherry tomatoes

Combine marinade ingredients in a saucepan and add 1 cup water. Bring to a boil. Reduce heat and simmer 20 minutes. Cool. Add meat and refrigerate overnight.

Drain meat, reserving marinade. Thread meat and vegetables alternately on skewers. Grill over medium coals 20 to 25 minutes, turning once. Brush with marinade 2 or 3 times during grilling.

Bring remaining marinade to a boil to serve with kabobs.

Serves 8

Note: Dip vegetables, except tomatoes, in very hot water for one minute to keep from splitting.

Savory Pot Roast

- 2 tablespoons olive oil
- 1 (3 1/2 – 4 pounds) beef round or chuck pot roast
- 1 (10-ounce) can cream of mushroom soup
- 1 (1-ounce) envelope dry onion soup mix
- 1 1/4 cups water
- 6 medium potatoes, quartered
- 6 carrots, cut into 2-inch pieces
- 2 tablespoons all-purpose flour

In a 6-quart Dutch oven heat oil and brown roast on all sides; skim fat. Stir in mushroom soup, soup mix and 1 cup water. Reduce heat to low; cover and cook 2 hours, stirring often.

Add vegetables; cover and cook 45 minutes or until roast and vegetables are fork-tender.

Remove roast and vegetables. Stir together flour and remaining water until smooth. Gradually stir into soup mixture. Cook until mixture boils and thickens, stirring constantly. Serve with roast.

Serves 8

Killer Filet of Beef

- 1 large beef filet, any size
- Salt and pepper to taste
- 1 tablespoon butter or oil
- 1 (10.5-ounce) can consommé
- 1/2 cup butter
- 3/4 bunch fresh parsley, long stems removed
- 2 cloves garlic, minced

The day before serving preheat oven to 425 degrees. Salt and pepper filet. In an ovenproof pan melt butter and brown meat. Place in oven 5 minutes; add consommé and return to oven 5 more minutes. Cool meat at room temperature, basting occasionally; refrigerate. When chilled, remove from refrigerator and cut into 1/4-inch slices.

In blender or food processor blend butter, parsley and garlic. Place 1 teaspoon butter mixture between each slice of meat and squeeze filet back together. Baste with consommé and return to refrigerator.

Preheat oven to 450 degrees. Bring meat to room temperature. Place filet in oven 7 minutes for medium rare or until cooked as desired. Serve immediately.

Serves 1 to 2

Susan's Old-Fashioned Meatloaf

Sauce

2 (8-ounce) cans tomato sauce
1/2 cup brown sugar
2 teaspoons cider vinegar
2 teaspoons prepared yellow mustard
3 teaspoons salt, or to taste

Meatloaf

2 pounds ground chuck or beef (not round)
1/4 cup crushed saltines
1/2 teaspoon pepper
1 teaspoon onion flakes or finely chopped onion
1/2 cup milk

Mix sauce ingredients together in a bowl.

Preheat oven to 350 degrees. Thoroughly combine meatloaf ingredients and add 2/3 of sauce. Mix together until totally incorporated. Do not put into meatloaf pans! Form meat into two long narrow loaves. Place loaves on broiler rack of a roasting or broiler pan. Bake 10-15 minutes.

Remove from oven and spread remaining sauce on tops and sides of loaves. Bake 1 hour; baste with sauce. Bake 15-25 minutes, until ends and edges of loaves are slightly browned. Slice and enjoy. Great cold in sandwiches.

Serves 8

Szeckley Goulash

2 pounds pork or beef cut in 1-inch cubes (lean pork loin roast or beef short ribs meat)
1 1/2 pounds sauerkraut, lightly rinsed
1 cup dark raisins
1 tablespoon caraway seeds
1 (15-ounce) can tomato sauce
2 tablespoons paprika

Combine all ingredients and cook in crock-pot all day on low or 3 hours in a 325-degree oven, tightly covered. Serve with boiled potatoes and sour cream.

Serves 4

Chinese Broiled Pork Tenderloin

2 (1-pound) pork tenderloins, short ends tucked under
1 tablespoon sherry
2 tablespoons soy sauce
1 1/2 teaspoons salt
1/2 teaspoon cinnamon
1/4 teaspoon ginger
1/4 teaspoon cloves
1 cup plum preserves
1/2 cup chutney
1 tablespoon sugar
1 tablespoon vinegar

Place pork in shallow dish and pour mixture of sherry, soy sauce and spices over it. Marinate 2 hours, turning occasionally.

Preheat oven to 450 degrees. Line broiler pan with foil and place rack on pan. Place pork on rack, reserving marinade. Brown pork 10 minutes. Baste with reserved marinade. Lower heat to 325 degrees and continue baking 30 to 45 minutes.

Mix preserves, chutney, sugar and vinegar until smooth. Serve tenderloin hot or cold with slightly warmed plum sauce.

Serves 4 to 6

Pork Tender Treats

Marinade

1/2 cup soy sauce
1 tablespoon minced onion
1/2 teaspoon garlic salt
1 tablespoon white vinegar
1/2 cup sugar
Dash pepper

3 (1-pound) whole pork tenderloins
1 pound bacon

Combine marinade ingredients.

Wrap tenderloins with bacon and place in 10 x 13-inch glass roasting pan. Pour marinade over meat; cover and place in refrigerator at least 2 hours or overnight. Turn occasionally.

Preheat oven to 300 degrees. Leave meat in marinade and bake, uncovered, 2 1/2 to 3 hours. Baste once or twice while baking. Pour sauce over slices when serving, if desired.

Serves 6 to 8

Pork Loin with Cranberry-Orange Sauce

1 boneless pork loin roast (4 - 6 pounds)
2 teaspoons cornstarch
1/4 teaspoon cinnamon
1/8 teaspoon salt
1 teaspoon grated orange peel
2 tablespoons orange juice
2 tablespoons dry sherry (cooking sherry)
1 (16-ounce) can whole berry cranberry sauce

Preheat oven to 325 degrees. Place pork loin on rack in baking pan. Roast 60 minutes.

Mix remaining ingredients in a small saucepan over low heat until mixture thickens. Pour 1/2 cup sauce over meat. Continue baking until meat thermometer registers 180 to 185 degrees. Total roasting time should be 35 to 40 minutes per pound. Serve remaining sauce on side.

Serves 6 to 8

Slow Cooked Ham

Prepare Ahead for a crowd.

1 (6-pound) bone-in ham
1 (8-ounce) jar yellow mustard
1 pound brown sugar

Place ham in Dutch oven or slow cooker, cover with water. Bring to a boil, reduce heat to low and simmer 8-10 hours. Remove and cool. (This should fall apart as you pick it up).

Pull ham into shreds and place in slow cooker. Stir in mustard and brown sugar, cover, and set to low. Cook until heated through. Serve on rolls as you would pulled pork.

Serves approximately 24

Note: Pineapple juice may be added to mustard sugar mix.

Ham Loaf with Horseradish Sauce

Ah! Comfort for a crowd.

2 pounds ground ham
1/2 pound ground pork
1/2 pound ground beef
1/2 cup quick oatmeal
1 cup whole milk
2 large eggs, whipped
3 tablespoons ketchup

Preheat oven to 350 degrees. Thoroughly mix ingredients and divide into 3 loaves. Place in 4 x 8-inch loaf pans. Bake 1 1 1/2 hours until loaves are browned; drain grease. Cool 30 minutes. Remove loaves from pans by inverting onto rimmed baking sheet; leave inverted. Baste all sides of loaves with sauce.

Basting Sauce

3/4 cup brown sugar
1/4 cup cider vinegar
1/4 cup water
1 teaspoon yellow mustard

Combine all ingredients and cook 10 minutes on low heat.

Bake basted loaves for an additional 30 minutes; basting occasionally. Cool slightly before serving.

Horseradish Sauce

1 cup mayonnaise, Hellmans recommended
1 cup sour cream
3/4 teaspoon seasoning salt
4 tablespoons horseradish sauce, slightly drained
1 teaspoon lemon juice
4 teaspoons fresh chopped parsley
2 teaspoons Dijon mustard
Salt and pepper to taste

Serve sauce as a side with sliced loaves.

Serves 15 to 20

Note: Loaves may be held or frozen before basting with sauce. Thaw before continuing recipe.

Macaroni and Cheese with Chicken

Michael Turner, Executive Chef, Classic Cup
301 West 47th Street, Kansas City, MO

2 chicken breasts
Vegetable oil
1 pound penne or cavatappi
1 quart whole milk
8 tablespoons unsalted butter
1/2 cup all-purpose flour
6 ounces Brie (1 1/2 cups)
8 ounces white Cheddar, grated (2 cups)
8 ounces yellow Cheddar, grated (2 cups)
Kosher salt
1/2 teaspoon freshly ground black pepper
1/2 teaspoon ground nutmeg
1 1/2 cups fresh white bread crumbs (5 slices, crusts removed)

Preheat oven to 350 degrees. Pan roast chicken breasts, chop and set aside.

Drizzle oil into a large pot of boiling salted water. Add pasta and cook according to package, 6 to 8 minutes. Drain well.

Heat milk in a small saucepan, do not boil. Melt 6 tablespoons butter in a 4-quart pot and add flour. Cook over low heat 2 minutes, stirring with a whisk. While whisking, add hot milk and cook until thickened and smooth. Remove from heat, add cheeses, chicken, salt, pepper and nutmeg; stir until cheeses melt. Add cooked macaroni and stir well. Pour into a 3-quart baking dish.

Melt remaining 2 tablespoons butter, combine with bread crumbs and sprinkle on top. Add a few bits of Brie.

Bake 35 to 45 minutes, until sauce is bubbly and macaroni is brown on top.

Serves 10 to 12

Chicken and Black Bean Enchiladas

3 cups chopped cooked chicken
1 (15-ounce) can black beans, rinsed and drained
1 (10-ounce) can diced tomatoes with green chilies
1 (8-ounce) can no-salt-added corn, drained
1 (8-ounce) package shredded Mexican 4-cheese blend
8 (8-inch) whole wheat flour tortillas
2 (10-ounce) cans enchilada sauce

Preheat oven to 350 degrees. Combine first 4 ingredients with 1 1/2 cups cheese in large bowl. Spoon chicken mixture down center of tortilla and roll up. Place seam side down in a 13 x 9-inch baking dish coated with cooking spray. Pour sauce over all, and top with remaining cheese. Bake covered 20 minutes, remove foil and bake 10 minutes more.

Serves 8 to 10

Chicken with Sherry and Olives

4 tablespoons white raisins
3/4 cup dry sherry
1 pound chicken tenders
3 tablespoons bread crumbs
3 tablespoons flour
4 tablespoons unsalted butter
Juice of 1 lemon
Salt and freshly ground pepper, to taste
20 black olives, pitted and chopped

Soak raisins in sherry 20 minutes. Drain and reserve both raisins and sherry.

Mix flour and bread crumbs. Cover tenders with saran wrap and pound until about 1/2-inch thick. Roll in crumb mixture to coat.

Heat butter in large skillet, add chicken a few pieces at a time, lightly brown both sides over medium heat and set aside. When all pieces are browned, return to skillet and add lemon juice, reserved sherry and salt and pepper. Cover and simmer over low heat 5 minutes, adding olives and raisins midway through cooking. Serve immediately with sherry-lemon sauce.

Serves 2 to 4

Sautéed Chicken with Olives, Capers and Roasted Lemons

1 cup extra-virgin olive oil (may need more or less)
6 lemons, sliced 1/4-inch thick
Salt and freshly ground black pepper, to taste
6-8 boneless, skinless chicken breast halves
1/2 cup all-purpose flour
3/4 cup pitted green Sicilian or Spanish olives, sliced
3-5 tablespoons capers, drained
3 cups chicken broth
3-4 tablespoons unsalted butter, cut into small pieces
4 tablespoons flat-leaf parsley, chopped

Preheat oven to 375 degrees. Line 1 or 2 baking sheets with parchment paper. Drizzle olive oil on paper, arrange lemon slices in single layer. Drizzle lemons lightly with oil and season with salt and pepper. Roast about 20 minutes, until edges begin to brown.

In a large deep skillet heat 1/2 cup oil. Season chicken with salt and pepper and dust lightly with flour; shake off excess. Cook over high heat, turning once, until golden (about 6 minutes); keep warm until all chicken is browned. Add capers, olives and broth, bring to a boil. Cook over high heat until stock is reduced, about 5 minutes. Add roasted lemons, butter and parsley; season with salt and pepper and simmer until chicken can be cut with a fork (or transfer pan to oven and cook at 275 degrees up to 3 hours). Transfer to serving dish and spoon sauce on top.

Serves 6 to 8

Swiss Chicken Casserole

4 cups cooked chicken or turkey, cut into bite-size pieces
1 medium onion, chopped
3-4 ribs celery, chopped
2 1/2 cups seasoned croutons
2 cups grated Swiss cheese
1 1/2 cups mayonnaise
1 cup sour cream
2 cups or (16-ounce) package dry buttermilk ranch dressing mix
1/2 cup toasted slivered almonds

Preheat oven to 325 degrees. Combine chicken, onion, celery, croutons and cheese. In a separate bowl mix mayonnaise, sour cream and dressing. Thoroughly combine the two mixtures. Spoon into a prepared 2-quart oblong baking dish (or similar 2-quart dish). Bake 40 minutes. Sprinkle top with almonds and bake an additional 10 minutes.

Serves 8 to 10

Turkey Meatloaf with Roasted Vegetables

1 onion, finely chopped
1 garlic clove, finely chopped
1 tablespoon olive oil
1 teaspoon salt
1/2 teaspoon pepper
1/3 cup Worcestershire sauce
1/2 cup chicken broth
2 teaspoons tomato paste
1 pound ground turkey breast
1 pound ground turkey, dark and breast meat
3/4 cup plain dry bread crumbs
2 eggs, beaten
1/2 cup barbeque sauce
1/2 cup ketchup
Baby Carrots
New potatoes, cut up
Olive oil
Seasoning salt

Preheat oven to 325 degrees. Sauté onions and garlic in olive oil until tender; add salt and pepper, Worcestershire sauce, chicken broth and tomato paste; mix well. Let cool to room temperature.

Combine ground turkeys, bread crumbs, eggs and cooled onion mixture. Mix well. Form loaf on baking pan. Mix barbeque sauce with ketchup and spread over turkey loaf. Place potatoes and carrots along turkey loaf, drizzle with olive oil and sprinkle with seasoning salt. Bake1 hour.

Note: Garlic mashed potatoes may be substituted for vegetables.

Serves 8 to 10

Chicken Piccata

- 4 skinless, boneless chicken breasts, halved
- 1/2 teaspoon sea salt
- 1/2 teaspoon freshly ground black pepper
- All-purpose flour, for dredging
- 4 tablespoons unsalted butter
- 2 tablespoons extra-virgin olive oil
- 1 shallot, finely chopped
- 1 garlic clove, finely chopped
- 1/2 cup dry white wine
- 1/2 cup reduced-sodium chicken broth
- 1/2 cup fresh lemon juice (from about 2 lemons)
- 1/4 cup drained capers, rinsed
- 1 tablespoon rosemary
- 1 tablespoon thyme
- 2 tablespoons chopped fresh flat-leaf parsley

Sprinkle chicken with salt and pepper and dredge in flour to lightly coat. In a large sauté pan melt 2 tablespoons butter with oil over medium-high heat. Add chicken and cook just until brown, about 3 minutes per side. Using tongs, transfer chicken to a plate. Add shallot and garlic to pan, lightly sauté; do not overcook. Remove to plate. Add wine and deglaze.

Place shallot, garlic, broth, lemon juice and capers back in pan. Bring broth mixture to a boil over medium-high heat, scraping up brown bits from bottom of pan for extra flavor. Return chicken to pan and simmer until just cooked through, about 5 minutes. Transfer chicken to a platter. Whisk remaining 2 tablespoons butter into sauce, add rosemary and thyme. Pour sauce over chicken, garnish with parsley and serve.

Serves 4 to 6

Phyllo Chicken Packets

3/4 cup chopped green onion
3/4 cup mayonnaise
3 tablespoons lemon juice
3/4 teaspoon dry tarragon
3 cloves garlic, minced or pressed, divided
2/3 cup butter
12 sheets phyllo dough, defrosted
6 boneless, skinless chicken breast halves
Salt and pepper to taste
2 tablespoons grated Parmesan

Preheat oven to 375 degrees. Mix together onion, mayonnaise, lemon juice, tarragon and 2 cloves garlic; set aside. Melt butter and add remaining garlic. For each packet, brush one sheet of dough with melted butter. Place second sheet on top and brush with butter. Sprinkle chicken with salt and pepper and place on phyllo. Spread one side of chicken with mayonnaise mixture, turn over on phyllo sheets and spread more on other side of chicken. Fold phyllo over chicken, envelope style, or twist corners together to make bunny ears.

Place packets on plain baking sheet and sprinkle with Parmesan. Bake 30 minutes.

Note: Be sure to keep phyllo dough covered with a damp cloth while working.

Serves 6

Baked Chicken à la Mesner

Paul Mesner, puppeteer

1 cup flour
2 tablespoons black pepper
1 tablespoon white pepper
2 tablespoons paprika
1/4 teaspoon cayenne pepper
1 tablespoon poultry seasoning
1 teaspoon chopped rosemary
1 tablespoon salt
1/2 teaspoon marjoram, thyme and oregano
4 chicken breast halves
4 chicken thighs

Preheat oven to 425 degrees. Combine all seasoning ingredients and dredge chicken pieces. Place in pan prepared with Pam and bake 1 hour. Should be crispy.

Serves: 4 to 8

Note: Fat from the skins of chicken gives this dish flavor; the dish almost has the appearance of fried chicken.

Rotisserie Chicken and Rice

1 cup white rice, cooked, cooled and dried
1 rotisserie chicken, shredded (4 cups)
1 (15-ounce) can black beans
3-4 plum tomatoes, chopped
4-5 scallions, chopped
1/2 (4-ounce) can chopped green chilies
1/4 cup white wine vinegar
3 tablespoons olive oil
3/4-1 teaspoon cumin

Mix all ingredients and serve at room temperature or cold.

Serves 4 to 6

Asian Rotisserie Chicken Salad

2 cups fresh cilantro leaves and soft stems
1/4 cup fresh lime juice (2 limes)
1/4 cup vegetable or olive oil
Coarse salt and ground pepper
1 rotisserie chicken, shredded (bones and skin removed)
1/4 medium head red cabbage, shredded
1 red bell pepper, thinly sliced
2 green onions, sliced
1 head romaine, torn into bite-size pieces
1/2 cup cashews

For dressing: combine cilantro, lime juice and oil in a blender; season with salt and pepper, blend.

In large bowl, combine chicken, cabbage, bell pepper and green onions; season with salt and pepper.

In a separate bowl, toss lettuce with 1/2 cup dressing. Divide among four serving plates and top with chicken mixture. Drizzle all with remaining dressing and sprinkle with cashews. All ingredients can be combined in one large serving bowl.

Serves 4 to 6

Asian Salad with Chicken

Paul Mesner, puppeteer

1/4 head of lettuce, torn into bite- sized pieces, per person
1/2 bunch cilantro, chopped
1-2 carrots, grated
Radishes, sliced (optional)
Red cabbage, shredded (optional)
Cucumber, peeled and seeded (optional)
1/2-3/4 cup Sichuan peanut sauce
1/2 chicken breast, cooked and sliced, (can be rotisserie) per person
Juice of 1 lime
Tortilla chips or strips

Combine lettuce with cilantro and vegetables. Combine peanut sauce with lime juice; pour over mixture and toss to mix. Top with chicken and tortilla chips or strips.

Thai Rotisserie Chicken and Noodle Salad

6 ounces uncooked rice noodles
2 cups cubed skinless, boneless rotisserie chicken
3/4 cup julienne carrots
3/4 cup chopped green bell pepper
1/2 cup chopped green onions, include tops
1/2 (8-ounce) can sliced water chestnuts, drained
1/4 cup Thai sweet chili sauce
2 tablespoons canola oil
2 tablespoons rice wine vinegar
2 tablespoons fresh lemon or lime juice
2 teaspoons low sodium soy sauce
1 teaspoon fresh ginger, peeled and grated
2 tablespoons unsalted dry roasted peanuts, chopped

Prepare noodles according to package directions, drain and cool. In large bowl combine noodles, chicken, carrots, bell pepper, onions and water chestnuts; toss well.

Whisk together chili sauce, oil, vinegar, juice, soy sauce and ginger in a small bowl. Drizzle mixture over noodle mixture; toss gently to coast. Sprinkle with peanuts. Serve immediately.

Serves 4

Note: a wedge of lime or lemon on the side looks and tastes good.

Shrimp and Broccoli Mornay

Sauce

4 tablespoons butter
4 tablespoons flour
1 1/2 cups milk or chicken stock
1/2 cup heavy cream
3/4 cup Gruyère cheese, grated
1/4 teaspoon salt
1/4 teaspoon pepper
Dash paprika

Melt butter in a heavy saucepan, add flour and cook, stirring, over low heat 3 minutes. Raise heat to medium and slowly add milk or stock and cream, whisking constantly until sauce begins to thicken, about 3 minutes. Slowly whisk in Gruyère. When cheese is incorporated, stir in salt, pepper and paprika. Stir well and remove from heat.

Shrimp and Broccoli

1 1/2 pounds fresh broccoli, steamed
1 1/2 pounds medium shrimp, peeled and deveined
2 tablespoons butter

Sauté shrimp in 2 tablespoons butter until pink and almost cooked (it will continue cooking after it is removed from heat). Place broccoli on platter and arrange shrimp on top; pour Mornay sauce over all.

Serves 6

Note: If sauce is too thick, thin with up to 1/2 cup cream.

Quick Sauce for Fish

1/2 cup sour cream
1/4 cup mayonnaise
2 teaspoons Dijon mustard
1 1/2 tablespoons grated fresh ginger
1 teaspoon orange zest
2 tablespoons fresh orange juice
1 1/2 tablespoons green peppercorns, drained
1/2 teaspoon sugar
1 tablespoon white wine vinegar
4 salmon or other fish fillets

Combine sauce ingredients and chill. Poach, grill or bake fish fillets and serve with sauce.

Serves 4

Sautéed Trout with Pecans

- 4 trout fillets with skin
- 1/4 teaspoon cayenne pepper
- 3/4 teaspoon salt, divided
- 3/8 teaspoon black pepper, divided
- 1/2 cup all-purpose flour
- 10 ounces unsalted butter, divided
- 3/4 cup pecans, chopped
- 2 tablespoons fresh lemon juice
- 1/3 cup chopped parsley

Pat fillets dry and rub flesh sides with cayenne, 1/2 teaspoon salt and 1/4 teaspoon black pepper. Dredge in flour. Heat 4 ounces butter in 12-inch heavy skillet over medium heat until foam subsides. Cook trout, skin side down, until skin is golden brown, about 4 minutes. Turn over and cook until just cooked through, 1 to 2 minutes more. Transfer to plate with slotted spatula. Keep warm, loosely covered with foil.

Pour butter from skillet and wipe clean. Cook pecans with remaining 6 ounces butter, 1/4 teaspoon salt and 1/8 teaspoon pepper over medium heat, stirring occasionally, until golden-brown, about 2 minutes. Stir in lemon juice and parsley and spoon over trout.

Serves 4

Wild Salmon with Gribiche

Ted Habiger, Room 39
1719 West 39th Street, Kansas City, MO

Sauce

- 1 egg, cooked hard
- 1 shallot, minced
- 2 tablespoons chopped parsley
- 1 tablespoon chopped tarragon
- 2 tablespoons chopped chives
- Zest of 1/2 lemon
- 1 tablespoon capers, rinsed, drained and chopped
- 3 gherkins, chopped fine
- 3/4 cup extra virgin olive oil
- Kosher or sea salt
- 4 (6-ounce) salmon fillets

In a small mixing bowl combine shallot, parsley, tarragon, chives, zest, capers, gherkins and olive oil. Season with salt. Chop egg white and egg yolk separately and add to mixture. Spoon over cooked salmon and serve.

Make sauce before cooking fish. Salmon can be eaten very rare and does not take long to cook. We prefer to grill our salmon, but basic principles apply for any cooking method. Season fish with salt and fresh cracked pepper and grill on hot grill approximately 3 minutes per side.

Oriental Salmon

Marinade:

2 tablespoons Dijon mustard
3 tablespoons soy sauce
6 tablespoons olive oil

1 1/4 pounds salmon fillets
1/2 teaspoon minced garlic
1/2 teaspoon minced ginger

Whisk together marinade ingredients in small bowl. Pour half the marinade over salmon and allow to set 5 minutes. Place skin side down on hot grill and cook 5 minutes per side. Remove from grill, pour remaining marinade over, and allow to rest 10 minutes before serving.

Serves 4 to 6

Grilled Leg of Lamb

Green Dirt Farm, Weston, Missouri

Marinade:

1/4 cup Dijon mustard
1/4 cup olive oil
1/4 cup red wine
1/4 cup fresh rosemary leaves, chopped
4 cloves garlic, minced
2 tablespoons coarse salt
2 tablespoons freshly ground black pepper

1 5-pound whole butterflied leg of lamb

Open lamb to lay flat.

Combine marinade ingredients and pour over lamb, rubbing all sides with your fingertips or the back of a spoon. Cover tightly and marinate overnight in refrigerator.

Prepare coals for grilling. When coals are still red hot, place meat 4-5 inches above coals. Turn and sear each side until all areas of lamb are brown or charred. (Don't worry if lamb chars, it will still taste fabulous). Raise lamb so that it is 6-8 inches off coals and allow to roast, covered. Turn it every 10 minutes or so, until a meat thermometer inserted in thickest part of leg registers 130 degrees for medium, 140 for medium-well, or 150 for well-done. This should take 20-30 minutes. Allow lamb to sit undisturbed, covered loosely by aluminum foil, 5-10 minutes before slicing.

Serves 6 to 8

Roast Lamb with Two Sauces

Red Wine Black Bean Sauce

1 cup dried black beans, picked over and rinsed
2 tablespoons chopped onion
2 tablespoons minced shallot
1/2 cup heavy cream
1 bay leaf
Pinch thyme
Pinch oregano
3 cups chicken broth, or as needed
1/3 cup Madeira or port
1/3 cup red wine
2 tablespoons butter, softened

Bean Sauce: Soak beans overnight in a medium pot. On the day of serving, drain beans and return to pot. Add onions, shallots, cream, bay leaf, thyme and oregano; pour in enough chicken broth to cover. Bring to a boil, reduce heat, cover, and simmer until beans are very tender. Puree in a blender or food processor, adding a little chicken broth if sauce is too thick. Strain through a fine sieve. Pour wines into pot; bring to a boil. Add bean puree and simmer 5 minutes; keep sauce hot.

Lamb Fillet

2-3 pounds lamb tenderloin
Salt
2 teaspoons crushed black and white peppers, combined
3 tablespoons vegetable oil

Lamb: Preheat oven to 375 degrees. Salt lamb on all sides; roll in crushed pepper to coat. Heat a large heavy skillet until very hot. Add oil; brown lamb on all sides. Transfer to a shallow baking pan; place in oven and bake 8 minutes for rare, 12-15 minutes for well-done. Remove from oven; cover and let stand 10 minutes to seal in juices before serving

Basil Sauce

3 tablespoons butter
1 tablespoon flour
1 cup chicken broth
1 clove garlic, minced
1 bunch fresh basil, washed, dried, stems removed

Basil Sauce: While lamb is baking, melt butter in a small sauce pan over medium heat and whisk in flour until well combined. Gradually add chicken broth; whisk until thickened. Remove from heat; add garlic and basil. Puree in a blender or food processor. Strain through a fine sieve; keep hot.

Just before serving whisk 2 tablespoons softened butter into black bean sauce; stir until butter melts. Carefully ladle some of sauce onto each of 4 or 6 plates, just to cover bottom of plate. Slice lamb into medallions; arrange in a fan shape on top of sauce. Make a thin line of basil sauce around lamb. Using a toothpick, swirl sauce decoratively.

Serves 4 to 6

Lamb Shanks Osso Buco Style

Green Dirt Farm, Weston, Missouri

2 tablespoons olive oil
4 lamb shanks sliced into 2-inch thick slices
2 medium onions
1 carrot, finely diced
2 tablespoons minced garlic
1 cup dry white wine
1 1/2 cups diced fresh tomatoes or diced canned tomatoes
2 cups lamb, beef or chicken stock
2-3 small strips lemon peel (only the zest – no white part)
1 bay leaf
1 teaspoon chopped fresh rosemary or 1/2 teaspoon dried
1 teaspoon chopped fresh thyme or oregano or 1/2 teaspoon dried
Salt and freshly ground black pepper

Gremolata

2-3 teaspoons lemon zest
2 cloves garlic, chopped
4 teaspoons fresh parsley, chopped
1/2 teaspoon freshly ground black pepper
Pinch of salt

Slow Cooker Method: In a large skillet heat oil over high heat. Add shanks and brown on all sides, turning often, 5-7 minutes. Remove meat and set aside. Pour off all but 2 tablespoons of fat from pan. Reduce heat, add onions and carrot and cook 10 minutes, stirring often, until vegetables are soft and a bit brown. Add garlic and cook 1 minute. Add wine, tomatoes and stock, bring to a boil, scraping up all brown bits from bottom of pan, until reduced by half. Put browned meat, lemon peel, bay leaf, rosemary, thyme or oregano and shanks into a slow cooker along with juices from skillet. Cook all day on low, until meat is falling off the bone.

Turn to high and leave cover off if there is too much sauce.

Oven Method: Preheat oven to 350 degrees. Brown meat in oil in a heavy bottomed pot or Dutch oven. Remove meat from pot and add onions and carrots. When these are soft and a bit brown add garlic and sauté for a minute. Add wine, tomatoes and stock and bring to a boil, scraping up browned bits. Return meat to pot along with zest and herbs. Cover pot and put in center of oven. Bake for 1 1/2-2 hours or until meat is quite tender. Remove shanks and cover to keep warm. Reduce sauce by half over high heat. Taste for salt and pepper. Return shanks to sauce.

Gremolata: Finely chop ingredients together by hand or in food processor. Gremolata will keep 2-4 hours refrigerated. When ready to serve, sprinkle gremolata generously over top of meat dish and serve with rice or pasta.

Serves 6

Madeira Braised Veal Jardinière with Whipped Yukon Potato

David Rogers, Executive Chef,
Restaurant Associates at the National Gallery of Art, Washington, DC

Veal

3 pounds veal loin
1 cup Madeira
1 medium onion, cubed
1 large carrot, sliced
3 stalks celery, sliced
4 garlic cloves
2 tablespoons tomato paste
6 sprigs fresh thyme
6 sprigs fresh rosemary
2 cups veal stock
Kosher salt
Freshly ground pepper

Vegetables

2 ounces olive oil
1 cup shiitake mushrooms
1 cup crimini mushrooms
12 baby carrots
1 cup pearl onions
2 cups sunburst patty pan squash
1 ounce butter
1 bunch chervil, washed, stems removed

Potatoes

6 Yukon gold potatoes
3/4 cup heavy cream
3/4 cup milk
4 ounces butter
Kosher salt and coarsely ground black pepper

To cook veal

Purchase veal loin already tied from butcher. Preheat oven to 350 degrees. Season veal loin on all sides with liberal amount of salt and pepper. In Dutch oven sear tied veal loin on all sides until well browned. Remove veal and set aside. Add carrot, celery, onion and garlic to Dutch oven and cook 5 minutes, or until vegetables are soft. Place veal back in pan. Add Madeira, tomato paste, veal stock and herbs. Bring to boil. Cover tightly with foil. Place in oven and braise, turning every 30 minutes, until veal is tender when pierced with a knife, about 2 hours. Once veal is cooked, remove and set on carving board to rest. Strain liquid through a chinois and season to taste with salt and pepper.

To cook vegetables

Bring a large pot of salted water to a boil. Remove stems from shiitake mushrooms. Peel baby carrots and trim tops, leaving a little green attached. Clean pearl onions. Trim patty pan squash, removing any stems. Blanch baby carrots and

(Continued on next page)

Madeira Braised Veal Jardinière with Whipped Yukon Potato *(continued)*

squash together in boiling water 3 minutes, remove and set aside. Heat olive oil in large sauté pan over medium heat. Add mushrooms and pearl onions and cook until caramelized; add baby carrots and squash. Remove pan from heat and stir in butter and chervil.

To cook potatoes
Peel potatoes, place in large pot with salted water and boil until tender when pierced with a knife. In separate pot bring milk and cream to a simmer, taking care not to boil. Add butter to hot cream mixture and let it melt. Strain potatoes and place in bowl of a stand mixer with paddle attachment. Gradually add cream mixture and mix until potatoes are smooth. Season with salt and pepper.

To serve
Place a small amount of potatoes in the middle of plate. Arrange vegetables around potatoes. Remove twine from veal. Slice veal and lean 1 or 2 slices against potatoes. Ladle finished sauce over veal and serve. Garnish potatoes with small sprigs of rosemary and thyme.

Serves 6 to 8

Veal Parmigiana

- 1 1/2 pounds thinly sliced veal (scallopine)
- 2 eggs
- Salt and pepper
- Flour for dredging
- Plain bread crumbs for dredging
- 1/4 cup olive oil
- 1 cup marinara sauce
- 1/2 cup shredded mozzarella cheese
- 2 tablespoons shredded Parmesan cheese

Preheat oven to 450 degrees. Lightly beat eggs. Place seasoned flour and crumbs in separate dishes for breading. Heat olive oil in a large skillet over medium heat. Dredge cutlets, in flour, one at a time, then dip in eggs and dredge in bread crumbs. Add to the skillet as they are ready. Turn cutlets as soon as browned. Total cooking time should be 5 minutes or less

Place all browned cutlets in a baking dish, do not overlap. Top each with a spoonful or two of sauce and add cheeses. Place baking dish in oven, baking until cheese melts. Serve immediately.

Serves 8

Shrimp and Asparagus in Bow-Tie Pasta

2 pounds uncooked shrimp, peeled, tails off
1/2 cup fresh lemon juice
2-3 tablespoons olive oil
Salt and pepper to taste
1 (16-ounce) package bow-tie pasta, cooked al dente
3/4-1 cup sun-dried tomatoes, cut into slivers
1 (3 1/2-ounce) jar capers
1/2 cup pine nuts, toasted
1 pound fresh asparagus, 2-inch pieces, steamed until crisp-tender
1/3 cup pitted kalamata olives, halved
6 tablespoons butter, melted
Zest of 1 large lemon
1/2 cup feta cheese, crumbled

Place uncooked shrimp in a non-reactive bowl and marinate in 1/4 cup lemon juice, olive oil, salt and pepper for up to 1 hour.

In a large bowl, combine cooked pasta, sun-dried tomatoes, capers, pine nuts, asparagus and olives. Stir lightly to mix ingredients. (This can be done up to 1 hour ahead of serving time).

Just before serving, cook shrimp on grill over a medium-hot fire until pink and a bit brown. Add shrimp, melted butter, remaining lemon juice, lemon zest and feta to pasta mixture. Toss to mix all ingredients, stirring up from bottom to get all small ingredients mixed thoroughly. Serve immediately.

Note: It is suggested to use a wire container (grill wok) to cook shrimp.

Million Dollar Spaghetti

2 (8-ounce) cans tomato sauce
Salt and pepper to taste
1 1/2 pounds ground beef, browned
1 (7-ounce) package vermicelli
1 (8-ounce) package cream cheese (light, if desired) softened
1/2 -3/4 pound cottage cheese
1/2 cup sour cream
1/2 cup chopped or sliced scallions
1/2 cup chopped green pepper

Preheat oven to 350 degrees. Add tomato sauce, salt and pepper to the meat and simmer while preparing remainder of dish. Cook vermicelli in salted water until al dente (it will cook more in casserole). Blend cheeses and sour cream; add scallions and green pepper to cheese mixture.

In a 2-quart casserole layer half of vermicelli, all of cheese mixture, remaining vermicelli and ending with meat mixture. Bake 45 minutes.

Can be refrigerated, but bring to room temperature before baking. Do not cover.

Serves 6

Rigatoni

1 (16-ounce) package rigatoni noodles

Sauce

2 large onions, chopped
Olive oil
4 cloves garlic
2 (12-ounce) cans tomato paste
8 cans water
1 (29-ounce) can tomato puree
1/2 cup sugar
4 dried red peppers, crumbled, or 4 teaspoons crushed red pepper
Salt and pepper to taste
1 pound hot pork sausage
1 pound Italian link sausage, cut into rings or chunks
1 tablespoon fennel seeds (optional)
2 cups shredded Parmesan cheese

Cook rigatoni until al dente. This will soften slightly when baked.

Sauté onion in oil; add garlic. Add remaining sauce ingredients, and simmer uncovered 2 hours.

Preheat oven to 350 degrees. Brown sausages and add fennel seeds, if desired. Drain off fat.

In a 4-quart deep casserole or 2 smaller casseroles assemble as lasagna: sauce, rigatoni, sausage, sauce and cheese. Repeat all layers, ending with cheese on top.

Bake uncovered approximately 30-45 minutes or until it bubbles.

Serves 8 to 10

Fresh Tomato Tart

5-6 fresh tomatoes, thinly sliced
1 small onion, grated
1 cup fresh chopped basil or 1/2 cup pesto
Salt and pepper to taste
1 cup grated sharp Cracker Barrel Cheddar cheese
1 cup grated Gruyère cheese
1 cup mayonnaise (1/2 light and 1/2 regular)
1 10-inch partially baked pie crust

Preheat oven to 375 degrees. Mix tomatoes, onion, basil or pesto, salt and pepper.

Mix cheeses and mayonnaise.

Place tomato mixture in pie shell and top with cheese mixture. Bake 30-35 minutes or until brown on top and bubbly. Slice and serve.

Serves 6

Rice and Lentil Pilaf

1/2 cup lentils, picked over, rinsed, drained
2 teaspoons olive oil
1 onion, chopped
4 garlic cloves, chopped
2 teaspoons curry powder
1/2 teaspoon ground cumin
1 cup basmati or jasmine rice
1 3/4 cups vegetable broth
1/2 teaspoon salt
2 tablespoons chopped cilantro
1 1/2 tablespoons fresh lemon juice
1 cup Greek-style plain yogurt (or low-fat plain yogurt)
1 cup toasted pine nuts

In a medium saucepan bring 4 cups water to a boil; add lentils, reduce heat and simmer 10 minutes. Drain well. In a large saucepan heat oil and sauté onion until softened. Add garlic, curry and cumin; cook, stirring until fragrant, about 1 minute. Stir in rice and lentils; cook, stirring, until thoroughly coated, 1-2 minutes. Stir in broth and salt; bring to a boil, then reduce heat and cook covered until liquid is absorbed, about 15 minutes. Let stand 5 minutes, sprinkle with cilantro and lemon juice and top with yogurt and pine nuts.

Serves 4

Tip
Microwave lemons, limes or oranges for 15-20 seconds, then roll, to obtain the maximum juice when squeezing.

Stuffed Cabbage Mollicone

- 12 large cabbage leaves
- 1 (15-ounce) can tomato sauce
- 1/4 cup lemon juice
- 1/2 cup sugar
- 1 pound fresh white mushrooms, coarsely chopped
- 1 large onion, diced
- 2 eggs, beaten
- 1 cup matzo meal
- Salt and pepper

Preheat oven to 350 degrees. Carefully cut around base of a head of cabbage to loosen leaves without removing core. Place whole head of cabbage in boiling water for a few minutes. Carefully remove outer leaves from head as they soften. Repeat until you have about 12 leaves. Return leaves to boiling water 3 minutes to soften. Save remainder of cabbage for soup or other dishes.

In a separate bowl gradually combine tomato sauce, lemon juice and sugar.

In a large mixing bowl combine mushrooms, onion, eggs and matzo meal. Add half of sauce mixture to thoroughly moisten and mix well. Reserve remaining sauce.

Place about 2 heaping tablespoons of mushroom mixture in each cabbage leaf and roll up. Place rolls in a shallow baking pan, cover with remaining tomato mixture (add another 8 ounces of tomato sauce, if desired) and bake for 90 minutes, basting several times.

Serves 6

Vegetable Lasagna Roll-Ups

Sauce

- 2 tablespoons canola oil
- 1 onion, chopped
- 2 carrots, peeled and chopped
- 3 stalks celery, chopped
- 2-3 cloves garlic, thinly sliced
- 3 tablespoons fresh basil or 1 tablespoon dried
- Ground black pepper
- 1 bay leaf
- 1/2 cup Madeira wine
- 2 1/2 cups low-sodium V-8 juice
- 1 (15-ounce) can chopped tomatoes
- 2 tablespoons tomato paste
- 1/2 cup applesauce
- Freshly grated Parmesan cheese

Lasagna

- 10-12 lasagna noodles
- 1 pound part-skim ricotta cheese
- 6 ounces part-skim mozzarella, shredded
- 2-3 broccoli stalks, steamed for 5 minutes (about 2 cups, cut up and chopped)
- 3 scallions, trimmed and chopped
- 2 tablespoons chopped fresh basil or 2 teaspoons dried
- 1 tablespoon chopped fresh oregano or 1 teaspoon dried

Sauce: Sauté onion, carrot and celery in oil in a large heavy-bottomed saucepan over medium heat, stirring frequently, about 2 minutes. Add garlic and cook 1 more minute. Stir in basil, pepper, bay leaf and Madeira; bring to a boil and cook until reduced by half, 2 or 3 minutes. Add rest of sauce ingredients except Parmesan. Reduce heat and simmer about 30-40 minutes. Remove bay leaf. Puree sauce or can leave chunky. Stir in Parmesan and set aside.

Lasagna: Preheat oven to 350 degrees. Add lasagna noodles to 4 quarts boiling water with 2 teaspoons salt. Test pasta after 12 minutes and cook until al dente. Drain and spread on a clean dish towel.

In a large bowl mix ricotta, mozzarella, broccoli, scallions, basil, oregano and parsley.

To assemble dish, spread 1 cup tomato sauce over bottom of greased 11x13-inch baking dish. Spread a noodle with approximately 1/3 to 1/2 cup of cheese/broccoli mixture; roll up strip. Place roll, seam side down, in baking dish. Repeat until all are completed. Pour rest of tomato sauce over rolls and cover pan tightly with aluminum foil. Bake 20 minutes; remove foil and bake 15-20 minutes more. Serve hot from pan, topped with prepared sauce.

Serves 8 to 10

Note: Sauce can be frozen; rolls can be frozen on a cookie sheet.

Tips From McGonigle's Market

Enjoy great steaks every time!

A Nice Hot Fire—Always start with a good HOT fire. This will sear in flavor and natural juices. It can be charcoal, gas, a broiler or a skillet, but start hot. When using charcoal allow flaming period to pass and use the hot glowing coals. Every grill is a little different, but generally 4-6 minutes on each side will produce a beautiful medium rare steak. Never use a fork or anything that will pierce the steak and allow juices to run out.

Seasoning or Marinade--In our taste tests we have found that our quality cuts of steak certainly do not need to be marinated for tenderness. It simply becomes a matter of taste. Just keep in mind that your goal is to enhance the steak flavor, not mask it. My favorite options are a dry steak seasoning or for the purist, just salt and pepper. Some studies even show that no seasoning at all actually produces the best beef flavor.

Steak Sauce—According to our founder, Bill McGonigle, you should never ruin a good steak with steak sauce. Try it pure and simple. We think you will love it. If you prefer sauce, try to stick with complimentary flavors that allow you to taste the rich goodness of a fine aged steak.

Desserts

Baby Cakes in the River Market, 108 E. Missouri, Kansas City, MO 64106

A Dessert Buffet – Menu Ideas

Desserts

Apricot Oat Squares

- 2 cups oatmeal, regular or quick
- 1 3/4 cups flour
- 1 cup butter, softened
- 3/4 cup brown sugar, packed
- 1 1/2 teaspoons cinnamon
- 1/2 teaspoon baking soda
- 1 (18-20-ounce) jar apricot preserves (Smuckers Simply Fruit suggested)
- 1/3 cup dried apricots, chopped

Preheat oven to 375 degrees and lightly grease a 9 x 13-inch pan. Mix all ingredients except preserves and apricots. Remove 2 cups mixture and set aside. Press remaining mixture into bottom of pan. Spread preserves and apricots on base. Crumble remaining mixture on top. Bake 25-35 minutes until lightly brown. Cool and cut. Store in a tightly covered container.

Fresh Berry Bruschetta

- 1 loaf French or Italian bread, sliced 1/2-3/4-inch thick
- 2 tablespoons butter, melted
- 1/4 cup superfine sugar
- 2 teaspoons cinnamon
- 1 (8-ounce) carton mascarpone cheese
- Assorted berries, rinsed and drained
- Honey
- Mint Leaves

Preheat oven to 375 degrees. Lightly brush both sides of bread slices with butter. Combine sugar and cinnamon, sprinkle on both sides of bread. Place on cookie sheet and bake/toast 10-12 minutes until crisp. Turn halfway through; cool.

To Serve: Spread each slice with mascarpone, top with berries and drizzle with honey. Garnish with mint if desired.

This is a good brunch dessert.

Note: Mix ricotta cheese with a small amount of lemon zest instead of using mascarpone.

Peanut Butter Sheet Cake

2 cups all-purpose flour
2 cups sugar
1 teaspoon baking soda
1/2 teaspoon salt
1 cup water
3/4 cup unsalted butter
1/2 cup peanut butter
1/4 cup vegetable oil
2 large eggs
1/2 cup buttermilk
1 1/2 teaspoons vanilla

Glaze

2/3 cup sugar
1/3 cup evaporated milk
1 tablespoon butter
1/3 cup peanut butter
1/3 cup miniature marshmallows
1/2 teaspoon vanilla

Preheat oven to 350 degrees. Combine flour, sugar, baking soda and salt and set aside.

Combine water and butter in saucepan and heat until boiling. Stir in peanut butter and oil and blend well. Add liquids to dry ingredients and mix well.

Combine eggs, buttermilk and vanilla; whisk to combine. Stir egg mixture into batter. Pour into a greased 10 x 15 x 1-inch pan. Bake 16-20 minutes or until pick inserted comes out clean.

Glaze: Combine sugar, milk and butter in saucepan; heat to a boil, stirring constantly, 2 minutes. Remove from heat and stir in peanut butter, marshmallows and vanilla; stir until melted. Spoon warm glaze over cake, spread to cover. Cool completely before cutting.

Makes 18 servings

Tip

Score brownies or dessert bars as soon as they are removed from oven. Cut with a plastic knife when cooled.

Gooey Butter Coconut Bars

First Layer

1 (18.5-ounce) Duncan Hines Butter Recipe Cake Mix
2 large eggs
1/2 cup butter, melted

Preheat oven to 325 degrees.

Mix cake mix, eggs and butter. Spread into lightly greased 9 x 13-inch glass baking dish.

Second Layer

1 cup flaked coconut
1 cup pecans, chopped

Sprinkle coconut and pecans and cover first layer.

Third Layer

1 (8-ounce) package cream cheese, softened
2 large eggs
3 1/2 cups confectioners sugar

Beat all ingredients together and spread carefully over top.

Bake 55 minutes, or until lightly brown.

Italian Cake

2 cups sugar
2 cups butter
5 egg yolks
2 teaspoons vanilla
5 cups flour
2 teaspoons cream of tartar
1 quart jam (strawberry, raspberry or peach)

Preheat oven to 300 degrees. Cream sugar and butter. Add egg yolks and vanilla. Stir in flour and cream of tartar. Mix until creamy but not stiff. Divide dough into two parts, about 3/4 and 1/4.

Line a jelly-roll pan (11 x 15-inch) with parchment paper, extending two inches beyond ends. Press larger amount of dough into the bottom of pan. Spread jam over dough.

Roll out remaining dough to the thickness of pie crust and cut into strips about 1/2 inch wide. Form diagonal stripes on top of jam.

Bake about 90 minutes until top is light golden brown. Cool, remove from pan and cut. Store in an air tight container.

Chocolate Crunch Bars

1 cup butter, softened
1 3/4 cups flour
1/2 cup sugar
1/4 teaspoon salt
2 cups semisweet chocolate chips (Ghiradelli suggested)
1 (14-ounce) can condensed milk
1 teaspoon vanilla
1 cup chopped pecans or walnuts

Preheat oven to 350 degrees. In large mixing bowl cream butter; beat in flour, sugar and salt until mixture is crumbly. With floured fingers press 2 cups of crumbs onto bottom of a lightly greased 9 x 13-inch pan; reserve remaining mixture. Bake on middle rack 10-12 minutes, until edges are golden brown.

Combine one cup chips with milk in heavy saucepan. Warm over low heat about 5 minutes, stirring until smooth and chocolate is melted; add vanilla. Spread chocolate over hot crust. Stir nuts and 1 cup chips with remaining crumb mixture and sprinkle over chocolate. Bake another 20-25 minutes. Cool in pan before cutting.

Note: Line pan with parchment paper extending over ends of pan for ease in removing bars.

Pecan Dream Bars

Tastes like a pecan pie.

Crust

1/2 cup butter
1/2 cup brown sugar
1 cup flour

Preheat oven to 350 degrees. Mix butter, sugar and flour and press into bottom of greased 9-inch square pan. Bake 15 minutes.

Filling

2 eggs
1 cup brown sugar
2 tablespoons flour
1/2 teaspoon baking powder
1 teaspoon vanilla
Pinch of salt
3/4 cup pecan halves

Mix all ingredients together and pour over cooked crust. Bake additional 30 minutes. Cool in pan and cut.

"Symphony Bar" Brownies

- 1 (17.6-ounce) Duncan Hines Brownie Mix with Walnuts
- 1 egg
- 1/4 cup water
- 1/4 cup canola oil
- 3 (6-ounce) Symphony candy bars with almond and toffee chips

Preheat oven to 350 degrees. Prepare mix according to directions using egg, water and oil.

Line a 13 x 9-inch cake pan with aluminum foil and cover with cooking spray. Spoon half of batter into pan and smooth with spatula. Place candy bars side by side on top of batter. Cover with remaining batter.

Bake 24-26 minutes. Let cool completely. Lift from pan using edges of foil. Serve slightly warm with vanilla ice cream, raspberry sauce and a sprig of mint.

Makes 24 large or 48 small brownies

Jim's Brownies

Jim Pittman, Black Tie Desserts

- 1/2 cup butter, melted
- 1 cup sugar
- 1 teaspoon vanilla
- 2 eggs
- 1/2 cup flour
- 1/4 teaspoon baking powder
- 1/3 cup cocoa
- 1/2 cup (generous) white chocolate chips
- 1/2 cup (generous) semisweet chocolate chips
- 1/2 cup (generous) walnut pieces
- Powdered sugar, optional

Preheat oven to 350 degrees. Mix together melted butter, sugar and vanilla; add eggs and stir. Mix dry ingredients together and add to butter mixture. Fold in chips and nuts. Bake in prepared 9 x 9-inch pan approximately 24 minutes. Do not over bake. Dust with powdered sugar if desired.

Buster Bar Dessert

1 (15-ounce) package chocolate sandwich cookies
1/2 cup butter, softened
1/2 gallon vanilla ice cream, softened
2 cups salted Spanish peanuts
2 cups powdered sugar, sifted
2/3 cup evaporated milk
1 cup chocolate chips
1/2 cup butter,

Crush cookies to size of coarse crumbs; mix with 1/2 cup butter and press into a 9 x 13-inch pan. Chill 1 hour or until firm. Spread ice cream over crust. Sprinkle with peanuts and return to freezer. Combine sugar, milk, chocolate chips and 1/2 cup butter and simmer 8 minutes. Cool thoroughly and spread over nuts. Freeze

Orange Brownies

1 3/4 cups flour
2 cups sugar
1 teaspoon salt
1 teaspoon baking powder
1 cup butter, softened
4 eggs
2 teaspoons pure orange extract
1 teaspoon grated orange zest.

Preheat oven to 350 degrees. Sift together flour, sugar, salt and baking powder. Add butter, eggs, extract and zest; beat with mixer until well blended. Pour into prepared 13 x 9-inch pan and bake 30 minutes, or until cake tests done. Pierce top of cake with fork.

Glaze

1 cup confectioners' sugar
2 tablespoons orange juice
1 teaspoon grated orange zest

Combine sugar, orange juice and zest, stirring until smooth. Pour over warm cake, cool before cutting.

Pike's Peak Spiked Apple Crisp

Ricki Creamer, Red Cedar Country Gardens
7895 West 183rd Street Stillwell, Kansas

5-6 cups Granny Smith apples, peeled, sliced
1/2 teaspoon cinnamon sugar
1 teaspoon gated lemon rind
1 teaspoon grated orange rind
1 jigger Grand Marnier
1 jigger Amaretto di Saronno
1/2 cup granulated sugar
1/4 cup light brown sugar, packed
3/4 cup sifted flour
1/4 teaspoon salt
1/2 cup butter
Whipped cream or ice cream

Preheat oven to 350 degrees. Pile apple slices very high in a 10-inch greased pie plate. Sprinkle cinnamon, lemon and orange rinds and both liqueurs on top of apples. In a separate bowl mix sugars, flour, salt and butter with pastry blender until crumbly. Spread mixture over top of apples. Bake uncovered until apples are tender and top is lightly browned, approximately 1 hour. Serve warm with topping of choice.

Serves 8

German Chocolate Angel Pie

A light dessert after a heavy meal.

2 egg whites
1/8 teaspoon salt
1/8 teaspoon cream of tartar
1/2 cup sugar
1/2 teaspoon vanilla
1/2 cup finely chopped pecans
1 (4-ounce) bar German sweet chocolate
3 tablespoons water
1 teaspoon vanilla
1 cup heavy cream

Preheat oven to 300 degrees. Beat egg whites with salt and cream of tartar until foamy. Add sugar 2 tablespoons at a time, beating well after each addition. Continue beating egg whites to stiff peaks. Fold in vanilla and nuts. Spoon into lightly greased 8-inch pie pan forming a shell; build sides up1/2-inch above edge of pan. Bake 50-55 minutes; cool.

Stir chocolate in water over low heat until melted. Cool until thickened and add vanilla. Whip cream, fold in chocolate mixture. Pile into shell. Chill 2 hours or more.

Serves 8

Summer Berry Mint Cream Tart

Shell

1/2 cup butter, room temperature
1/3 cup sugar
1/4 teaspoon salt
1/2 teaspoon vanilla
1 1/4 cups flour

Preheat oven to 375 degrees. Cream butter with sugar, salt and vanilla. Add flour and blend until crumbly. Firmly press crumb mixture into bottom and sides of buttered 10-inch tart pan. Chill 30 minutes. Prick shell with fork; line with foil and place beans or pie weights on shell. Bake in lower third of oven 15 minutes. Remove weights and foil and bake shell an additional 10 minutes or until golden. Cool on rack 5 minutes, remove from sides of pan and cool completely.

Filling

1 cup milk
1/3 cup fresh mint leaves, packed and chopped
3 large egg yolks
1/2 cup sugar
2 1/2-3 tablespoons cornstarch
1 teaspoon vanilla
3/4-1 cup heavy cream, chilled
1 quart strawberries, hulled
2 cups blueberries
1 cup raspberries

In small saucepan bring milk and mint leaves to boil. Remove pan from heat and let stand covered 5 minutes. Strain milk through fine sieve, pressing hard on mint. Whisk together egg yolk, sugar, cornstarch and vanilla. Whisk in strained milk and bring to boil over medium heat, whisking constantly. Simmer, while whisking, 3 minutes. Transfer to bowl and cover cream surface with plastic wrap and chill 4 hour or until firm. (Pastry cream may be made one day in advance. Keep covered and chilled).

In chilled bowl beat cream to stiff peaks. Whisk pastry cream until smooth and whisk in half of whipped cream. Gently fold in remaining whipped cream.

Place shell on serving platter and fill with mint cream. Stand strawberries, hull end down, around edge of crust. Scatter blueberries around, next raspberries. Chill 1 hour.

Shell and filling can be made a day ahead. Whip cream and add fruit the day it is served.

Serves 12

Note: This is not as difficult as it seems, if done in steps. It is a pretty and delicious summer dessert.

Chocolate Orange Tart

Crust

1 1/2 cups slivered almonds, toasted
1/4 cup brown sugar, packed
1/4 cup all-purpose flour
1/4 cup unsalted butter, melted

Preheat oven to 325 degrees. Combine almonds and brown sugar in food processor or blender and process a portion at a time until nuts are finely ground. Transfer to mixing bowl. Stir in flour and add butter, stirring until well combined. Press onto bottom and up 1 inch on sides of a 9-inch tart pan with removable bottom or 9-inch springform pan. Bake 20 minutes or until golden and firm to touch. Cool on wire rack.

Filling

3/4 cup whipping cream
6 ounces semi-sweet chocolate, chopped or 1 cup semi-sweet chocolate pieces
2 tablespoons Grand Marnier or brandy
1/3 cup orange marmalade
1 ounce white chocolate

In a small saucepan heat cream to simmering. Remove from heat; whisk in chocolate until smooth. Whisk in Grand Marnier or other liqueur (optional). Cool until thickens but pourable, about 30 minutes.

Spread marmalade over bottom of crust; pour filling over this. Cover and chill 20 minutes or until filling is not quite set. Using a vegetable peeler shave white chocolate and sprinkle over tart. Cover and chill 2 hours or until filling is firm; can be held overnight.

Serves 10 to 12

Tip

Toasting nuts: Spread nuts on a cookie sheet and place in a preheated 350 degree oven for 10 minutes; stir and return to oven and check every 3-5 minutes. Watch closely. They can be toasted in a dry skillet, again watch closely. Olive oil can be added for extra flavor

Light Blueberry Pie

- 2 cups blueberries, or other berries
- 4 egg whites
- 2/3 cup sugar
- 1 teaspoon vanilla
- Zest of 1 small lemon
- 1/4 teaspoon salt
- 1 tablespoon unflavored gelatin
- 1/4 cup cold water
- 1 cup heavy cream
- 1 (9-inch) graham cracker crust

Beat egg whites until they hold a peak. Slowly add sugar, vanilla, zest and salt and beat again until they hold a peak. Soften gelatin in water in top of double boiler. Heat water to dissolve gelatin; mix into egg mixture. Whip heavy cream to soft peaks and fold into mixture. Fold in blueberries; spoon into pie shell and refrigerate until set. Garnish with a strawberry "fan" or raspberries with a drizzle of diluted raspberry jam and a mint leaf.

Serves 8

Note: Egg Beaters egg whites can be used. Cool Whip may be substituted for heavy cream.

Grapefruit Baked Alaska

- 1 quart lime sherbet
- 3 large grapefruit, pink if available
- 6 large egg whites
- 1/4 teaspoon cream of tartar
- Pinch of salt
- 1/2 cup sugar

Line a cookie sheet with wax paper. Freeze 6 small scoops of sherbet.

Preheat oven to 425 degrees. Halve grapefruit crosswise and discard visible seeds. Cut segments free from membrane but do not remove them. Arrange fruit halves, cut side up, on baking sheet.

Beat egg whites with cream of tartar and salt until they just hold soft peaks. Gradually add sugar, beating on high until meringue is stiff and glossy.

Place sherbet on fruit halves; generously top with meringue, making sure you seal edges. Bake in middle of oven until meringue is golden, about 7-8 minutes.

Serve immediately.

Serves 6

Note: May remove grapefruit segments and mix with other fruit, return mixed fruit to grapefruit cups and continue with recipe.

Poached Pears in Zabaglione Sauce

8 Bosc or Bartlett pears, peeled, leaving stems
If using Bartletts, they should be firm
3 cups water
1 1/2 cups sugar
1 stick cinnamon
1 vanilla bean or 1 tablespoon vanilla

Combine water, vanilla bean, cinnamon and sugar, bring to a boil. When sugar is dissolved, add pears and simmer 25 minutes. Allow pears to cool in liquid. May be prepared ahead and stored in liquid.

Sauce

4 egg yolks
1/3 cup sugar
3/4 cup Cointreau
1 cup whipping cream, beat until firm

In top of double boiler whisk together yolks, sugar and Cointreau. Place over simmering water and whisk until sauce is thick and coats a metal spoon, about 15-20 minutes. Do not boil water as mixture may curdle. Transfer sauce to bowl and cool. Fold sauce into cream. Serve in bowl surrounded by sauce. Garnish with raspberries or mint, chocolate or holly leaves.

Serves: 8

Tip

To use a vanilla bean split bean in half, lengthwise, scrape out as much as possible of the contents. Place the remaining bean in sugar for vanilla flavored sugar.

Tip

To make chocolate leaves place small clean leaves on a sheet of foil, melt chocolate of your choice (chips are easiest). Brush chocolate on top of leaves. Let chocolate harden, carefully peel leaves away.

Peach Blueberry Tart

Pastry:

1 1/2 cups flour
1/2 cup sugar
1 teaspoon baking powder
1/4 teaspoon salt
1/2 cup cold butter, cubed
1 egg
1 teaspoon vanilla

In food processor pulse flour, sugar, baking powder and salt. Add butter and pulse just until mixture resembles coarse meal. Add egg and vanilla, pulse until dough clumps and begins to form a ball. Press dough onto bottom and sides of a 9-inch springform pan. Chill in pan until firm, about 10 minutes.

Filling

1/2 cup sugar
2 tablespoons flour
1 tablespoon quick-cooking tapioca
2 pounds firm-ripe peaches, pitted, sliced
1 cup blueberries
1 tablespoon fresh lemon juice

Preheat oven to 375 degrees. Pulse 2 tablespoons sugar with flour and tapioca until tapioca is pulverized. Transfer to large bowl and stir in remaining sugar. Add peaches, blueberries and lemon juice and gently toss to coat. Spoon filling into pastry and bake, loosely covered with foil, until filling is bubbling and crust is golden, about 1 1/2 hours.

Filling will set up as it cools. Cool, uncovered, 20 minutes, carefully remove side of pan.

Cool cake to barely warm or room temperature before cutting.

Serves 8 to 10

Raspberry Peach Crisp

4 large fresh peaches
1 pint fresh raspberries
1/2 cup sugar
2 tablespoons flour
1 cup oatmeal
1 cup brown sugar, packed
4 tablespoons butter
1 teaspoon cinnamon

Preheat oven to 350 degrees. Lightly grease 8-inch square dish or 10-inch pie plate. Place peach slices on bottom and cover with raspberries. Combine dry ingredients and mix well, cut in butter. Sprinkle over top of fruit. Bake 1 hour. Top with ice cream, if desired.

Serves 6

Rhubarb and Strawberry Crisp

Andrew Sloan, Room 39 at Mission Farms
10561 Mission Road, Leawood, Kansas

2.5 pounds rhubarb, peeled and chopped
2 pounds strawberries, stemmed and chopped
1/2 cup sugar

Crisp Topping
2 1/2 cups flour
1/2 cup pistachios, lightly toasted and ground
1/2 cup brown sugar, packed
1/2 cup sugar
1/2 teaspoon cinnamon
5 pods cardamom, ground
1/2 pound butter, melted and cooled

Preheat oven to 350 degrees. Combine rhubarb, strawberries and sugar in large bowl. In separate bowl, combine all crisp toppings except butter and whisk together. Slowly add butter but keep topping slightly dry. Divide the rhubarb mixture among ramekins and add topping. Bake for 25-30 minutes until fruit is bubbly and crisp is browned.

Makes 18 4-ounce servings

Easy Blueberry Crumble

The Berry Patch
22509 State Line Road, Cleveland, MO

4 cups fresh or frozen blueberries
1 cup sugar
2 cups flour
Dash of salt
1 cup butter
1/4 cup chopped pecans.

Preheat oven to 375 degrees. Butter a 9 x 13-inch or 9 x 9-inch pan or spray with oil. Spread blueberries in pan. Mix sugar, flour and salt. Cut in butter until crumbly. Sprinkle over berries. Sprinkle with pecans.

Bake for 45 minutes, or until light golden brown. Serve with ice cream or whipped cream.

Old Fashioned Caramel Layer Cake

Cake

Cooking spray
1 tablespoon flour
1 1/2 cups sugar
1/2 cup butter, softened
2 eggs
1 egg white
2 1/4 cups flour
2 1/2 teaspoons baking powder
Pinch of salt
1 1/4 cups milk
2 teaspoons vanilla

Preheat oven to 350 degrees. Spray two 9-inch cake pans, line bottoms with wax paper and spray again, dust with flour.

Beat sugar and butter on medium speed until well blended. Add eggs and egg white one at a time, beating well after each addition. Whisk together flour, baking powder and salt. Add flour mixture to sugar mixture, alternating with milk. Stir in vanilla. Pour batter into prepared pans and tap out bubbles. Bake 30 minutes or until center tests done. Cool 10 minutes, remove from pans and carefully peel off wax paper. Cool

Frosting

1 1/2 cups dark brown sugar, packed
3/4 cup milk
4 tablespoons butter
3 teaspoons corn syrup
Pinch of salt
3 cups powdered sugar
3 teaspoons vanilla

Combine brown sugar, milk, butter, corn syrup and salt in medium saucepan. Bring to boil over medium high heat, stirring constantly. Reduce heat and simmer, stirring occasionally, until thick (about 5 minutes). Remove from heat and add powdered sugar and vanilla. Beat at medium speed until smooth. Cool 2-3 minutes. (Frosting will be thin but thickens as it cools). Slice each cake into 2 layers.

Assemble: Place one layer on plate and frost. Repeat with all layers. Frost top and sides. Store loosely covered in refrigerator.

Serves 18

Chocolate Cake with Buttercream Frosting

Cake

1 cup water
1 cup butter
4 tablespoons cocoa powder
2 cups sugar
2 cups flour, sifted
1 teaspoon baking soda
2 eggs, room temperature
1 teaspoon vanilla
1/2 cup buttermilk

Preheat oven to 350 degrees. In a saucepan combine water, butter and cocoa and bring to a boil. Transfer to a mixing bowl and add remaining ingredients, adding eggs one at a time. Bake in 2 prepared pans approximately 25 minutes, until center tests done. Cool in pans 30 minutes. Turn out onto rack to cool completely before frosting.

Frosting

3 egg whites, pasteurized
Pinch of salt
2 1/2 cups powdered sugar
8 ounces butter
2 1/2 tablespoons Crisco
3 tablespoons cocoa powder
1/2 teaspoon vanilla

Whip egg whites with salt until stiff peaks form. Add 1 1/4 cups powdered sugar and mix. Combine remaining sugar, butter, Crisco, cocoa and vanilla. Beat until desired consistency.

Serves 10 to 12

Tip

Buttermilk can be made by adding 1 tablespoon white vinegar or lemon juice or cream of tartar to 1 cup of milk. Stir and allow to stand 15 minutes. When it starts to curdle, stir well. Powdered buttermilk is available in many grocery stores.

Nebraska City Cake

Cake

- 1/2 cup Crisco
- 2 cups sugar
- 2 eggs
- 2 cups flour
- 2 teaspoons baking soda
- 1 teaspoon salt
- 2 teaspoons ground cinnamon
- 1 teaspoon grated nutmeg
- 4 cups (about 6) Granny Smith apples, diced
- 1 cup chopped pecans or walnuts

Cake: Preheat oven to 350 degrees. Grease a 9 x 13-inch pan. Cream sugar and shortening, add eggs. Combine flour, soda, salt, cinnamon and nutmeg and add to sugar mixture. Stir in apples and nuts. (The mixture will be dry). Pour into pan and bake 50-60 minutes, until cake shrinks slightly from sides. Remove from oven and cool in pan on rack.

Sauce

- 1/2 cup butter
- 1 tablespoon flour
- 1/2 cup sugar
- 1/2 cup brown sugar, packed
- 1/2 cup half-and-half

Over low heat melt butter, gradually stir in flour and sugars; stir in half-and-half. Cook, stirring constantly, until thickened.

Cut cake into squares and serve topped with warm sauce.

Serves 24

Tip

To keep brown sugar from hardening place a slice of apple or bread in the bag. If sugar has hardened, a slice of bread will soften it again in a couple of hours.

Grand Finale Apple Cake

Cake

4 cups unpeeled apples, diced
2 cups sugar
3 cups flour
2 teaspoons baking soda
1 teaspoon salt
2 teaspoons cinnamon
1/2 teaspoon allspice
1/2 teaspoon nutmeg
1/2 teaspoon cloves
3/4 cup vegetable oil
2 eggs, beaten
1 tablespoon Worcestershire sauce
1 cup chopped nuts
1 cup raisins

Preheat oven to 325 degrees. Grease and flour a 12-cup bundt pan. In large bowl combine apples and sugar. Set aside 15 minutes. Sift together dry ingredients. Stir oil, eggs and Worcestershire into apple mixture; fold in flour mixture, nuts and raisins. Bake 1 hour and 15 minutes.

Glaze

1 cup sugar
2/3 cup lemon juice
Zest of 1 lemon

Simmer sugar and lemon until sugar dissolves, about 5 minutes. Poke hot cake with a skewer and pour glaze over cake.

Serves 16

Lemon Pudding Cake

4 eggs, separated
1/3 cup lemon juice
1 teaspoon lemon zest
1 tablespoon butter, melted
1 1/2 cups sugar
1/2 cup sifted flour
1/2 teaspoon salt
1 1/2 cups milk
Whipped cream, optional

Preheat oven to 350 degrees. Beat together egg yolks, lemon juice, zest and butter until thick. Combine sugar, flour and salt and add to egg mixture, alternating with milk and beating after each addition. Beat egg whites until stiff. Blend into batter using low speed on a hand mixer or by hand. Pour into 8-inch square baking dish. Set in a pan of hot water. Bake 45 minutes or until golden. Serve warm topped with cream, if desired.

Serves 8

Lucy Loom Cake

Ricki Creamer, Red Cedar Gardens
7895 West 183rd Street, Stilwell, KS

- 2 cups applesauce, unsweetened
- 2 teaspoons baking soda
- 1 cup butter, softened
- 2 cups sugar
- 2 eggs
- 2 teaspoons cinnamon
- 1 teaspoon nutmeg
- 1 teaspoon cloves
- 1 teaspoon allspice
- 2 1/2 cups flour
- 1/2 cup strawberry preserves
- 1 cup raisins
- 1 cup chopped toasted walnuts

Preheat oven to 350 degrees. Mix applesauce and baking soda, set aside. Cream butter and sugar, then beat in eggs. Sift flour and all spices and add to butter mixture. Stir in applesauce mixture. Add remaining ingredients. Pour into greased and floured bundt pan. Bake 1 hour or until tests done.

Serves 18

Note: This freezes well.

Chocolate Mousse Cake

- 3 (3-ounce) packages ladyfingers, split
- 1 cup sugar
- 1/2 cup heavy cream
- 1/4 cup butter
- 1 (8-ounce) package semi-sweet chocolate chips
- 1 teaspoon vanilla
- 1-2 teaspoons hazelnut liqueur, optional
- 2 cups heavy cream, whipped

Line bottom and sides of a 9-inch springform pan with ladyfingers, placing them close together. Cook sugar, 1/2 cup cream and butter in heavy saucepan over medium heat, stirring constantly, 5-7 minutes or until sugar dissolves. Add chocolate, vanilla and liqueur, if desired; stir until chocolate melts. Remove from heat and cool slightly. Fold whipped cream into chocolate mixture. Pour 1/3 of mixture into prepared pan, top with half of remaining ladyfingers. Repeat layers, ending with chocolate mixture. Chill at least 4 hours. Carefully remove sides of pan. Garnish with powdered sugar, raspberries or strawberries, if desired.

Serves 12

Note: May be frozen, covered, up to one month. Thaw in refrigerator 8 hours.

Individual Blueberry Coconut Pound Cakes

1/2 cup butter, softened
3/4 cup sugar
2 teaspoons lime zest
2 eggs
5 tablespoons heavy cream
1 cup flour
1/4 teaspoon salt
2/3 cup plus 3 tablespoons sweetened flaked coconut
1/2-3/4 cup blueberries

Preheat oven to 350 degrees. Butter and flour 9 muffin cups. Beat together butter, sugar and zest until light and fluffy. Beat in eggs, one at a time. Beat in cream then flour and salt on low speed until just combined. Stir in 2/3 cup coconut and gently fold in blueberries. Spoon batter into cups and smooth tops. Sprinkle with remaining coconut. Bake 25 minutes or until edges are golden brown. Invert and cool.

Makes 9

Lacy Oatmeal Cookies

l l/2 cups quick oats
1/2 cup butter, melted
3/4 cup sugar
l teaspoon flour
l teaspoon baking powder
l/3 teaspoon salt
l/2 teaspoon cinnamon
1-2 shakes nutmeg
l/2 cup chopped pecans
l egg
2 teaspoons vanilla

Preheat oven to 375 degrees. Cover cookie sheets with foil or parchment paper. In large bowl mix oats and melted butter. Combine next seven ingredients and add to oat mixture. Beat egg and vanilla, stir into mixture. Place teaspoonfuls of dough on cookie sheets. Bake 8-10 minutes. Let cool before removing from cookie sheet.

Makes 4 dozen

Chocolate Shortbread Cookies

- l/2 cup unsweetened cocoa powder
- l/4 teaspoon baking soda
- l/4 teaspoon salt
- l cup unsalted butter, softened
- l cup powdered sugar
- l l/2 teaspoons vanilla
- 2 cups flour

Preheat oven to 325 degrees. Cream butter in electric mixer; add sugar, a little at a time, and vanilla. Mix in dry ingredients at low speed (dough will be stiff). Place dough on large sheet of waxed paper and cover with another sheet; roll dough to l/3-inch thickness. Chill dough on baking sheet until firm, about 2 hours. (Will keep, wrapped, up to 2 days). Peel off top sheet and cut into shape of choice with cookie cutter. Arrange 2 inches apart on parchment lined baking sheet. Re-roll dough and continue. Bake 16-18 minutes. Cool on racks. Store in airtight container.

Makes about 50, depending on size of cutter

Lemon Crisps

Cookies

- 1 1/2 cups sugar
- 1 cup butter, softened
- 2 eggs
- 3 tablespoons sour cream
- 1/2 teaspoon lemon extract or 1 teaspoon vanilla
- l teaspoon lemon zest
- 3 l/4 cups flour
- l/2 teaspoon baking soda
- l/2 teaspoon salt
- Powdered sugar

Preheat oven to 375 degrees. Lightly grease cookie sheets. In large bowl beat sugar and butter until fluffy. Beat in eggs, sour cream, lemon extract or vanilla and zest. Combine flour, soda and salt and stir into sugar mixture. Chill. Sprinkle powdered sugar on pastry cloth or board. Roll out half of dough to 1/8 inch thickness. Cut out with cookie cutters. Repeat with remaining dough. Place 1 inch apart on cookie sheet. Bake 10-12 minutes until lightly browned. Cool on rack.

Glaze

- 2 cups powdered sugar
- 3 tablespoons lemon juice
- 3 teaspoons lemon zest

Heat powdered sugar and lemon juice over low heat. Add lemon zest and cool slightly. Add water to thin if needed. Drizzle glaze over cookies.

Makes 6 dozen

Brown Sugar Cookies

14 tablespoons unsalted butter
1/4 cup sugar
2 cups dark brown sugar
2 cups plus 2 tablespoons unbleached all-purpose flour
1/2 teaspoon baking soda
1/4 teaspoon baking powder
1/2 teaspoon salt
1 large egg
1 large egg yolk
1 tablespoon vanilla extract

Preheat oven to 350 degrees. Line two 18 x 12-inch baking sheets with parchment paper.

Heat 10 tablespoons butter in skillet (not nonstick) over medium-high heat until melted, about 2 minutes. Continue to cook until butter is dark golden brown and has a nutty aroma, 1-3 minutes. Remove from heat and pour into a bowl, stir remaining butter into hot butter to melt; set aside 15 minutes.

In shallow baking dish or pie plate mix granulated sugar and 1/4 cup brown sugar until well combined; set aside. Whisk flour, baking soda and baking powder together and set aside.

Add remaining brown sugar and salt to cooled butter; mix until no sugar lumps remain. Scrape down sides of bowl and add egg, yolk and vanilla; scrape down bowl, add flour mixture and mix until just combined.

Divide dough into 24 portions, each about 2 tablespoons, roll into balls about 1 1/2 inches in diameter. Roll balls in reserved sugar mixture to coat and set on sheet about 2 inches apart, 12 per sheet. (They will spread).

Bake in center of oven, one sheet at a time, until cookies are browned and still puffy and edges have begun to set but centers are still soft (cookies will look raw between cracks and seem underdone). Bake 12 to14 minutes, rotating baking sheet halfway through baking. DO NOT OVERBAKE. Cool on sheet for 5 minutes before transferring to wire rack to finish cooling.

Makes 24

Cranberry Double Chocolate Chip Cookies

Won first place in chocolate chip cookie bake off.

1 cup salted butter, melted and cooled
1 cup sugar
1 cup dark brown sugar
2 large eggs
2 teaspoons vanilla
2 cups all-purpose flour
2 1/2 cups rolled oats (not quick) ground until almost a fine flour
1/2 teaspoon salt
1 teaspoon baking powder
1 teaspoon baking soda
1 tablespoon whole milk
12 ounces white chocolate chips
12 ounces semisweet chocolate chips
1 1/2 cups dried cranberries

Preheat oven to 375 degrees. Mix butter and sugars until well blended. Mix eggs and vanilla and add to sugar mixture. Do not over beat. Blend flour, ground oatmeal, salt, baking powder and soda; add to wet ingredients 1/2 cup at a time until all is mixed in. Add milk, then chips and cranberries. Bake on lightly greased cookie sheets 10-12 minutes. (Watch carefully toward end. They will brown quickly).

Makes 36 cookies

Note: Jim Pittman of Black Tie Desserts suggests adding 1 cup coarsely chopped macadamia nuts.

Orange White Chocolate Chip Cookies

2 1/4 cups flour
3/4 teaspoon baking soda
1/4 teaspoon salt
1 cup butter
1/2 cup sugar
1/2 cup brown sugar
1 egg
1/2 teaspoon orange oil or
3/4 teaspoon orange extract and
1 teaspoon orange zest
2 cups white chocolate chips

Preheat oven to 350 degrees. Sift together flour, soda and salt. Cream butter and sugars; add egg, extract and zest until well blended. On low speed of mixer beat in dry ingredients and beat well. Stir in chips. Using a cookie scoop drop on baking sheet and bake 10 minutes.

Makes 36.

Note: Orange extract found at Williams Sonoma or Dean and Deluca.

Orange Carrot Cookies

Cookie

1 cup butter
3/4 cup sugar
1 egg, beaten
1 cup cooked, mashed carrots, chilled
2 cups flour
2 teaspoons baking powder
1/4 teaspoon salt
1/2 teaspoon vanilla
1/2 teaspoon almond extract

Preheat oven to 350 degrees. Cream butter and sugar; add egg and other ingredients in order given. Drop by teaspoonfuls onto greased cookie sheet. Bake 12-15 minutes.

Icing

3 tablespoons butter
2-3 cups powdered sugar, sifted
3-6 tablespoons orange juice
1 tablespoon orange zest

Mix together butter, sugar, orange juice and zest to desired consistency for icing. Ice cookies while still warm.

Makes 4 to 5 dozen

Mr. Fields' Chocolate Chip Cookies

- 1 cup unsalted butter, softened, do not substitute
- 1/2 cup sugar
- 1 1/2 cups brown sugar, packed
- 2 large eggs
- 2 1/2 teaspoons vanilla
- 3 1/4 cups all-purpose flour
- 1 tablespoon cocoa
- 1 teaspoon salt
- 1 1/2 teaspoons baking powder
- 1 1/2 teaspoons baking soda
- 18 ounces semisweet Ghiradelli chocolate chips
- 1-1 1/2cups chopped nuts of your choice

Preheat oven to 350 degrees. In large mixing bowl cream butter, eggs, sugars and vanilla. Mix together flour, cocoa, salt, baking powder and baking soda. Combine cream mixture with dry ingredients. Stir in chocolate chips. Place golf ball sized portions 2 inches apart on plain cookie sheet. Bake 9-10 minutes.

Makes 24 to 30

Tip

Table salt *is fine-grained refined salt with additives that make it free-flowing, is mainly used in cooking and as a table condiment.*
Iodized salt is table salt with added iodine, important in areas that lack natural iodine, an important preventative for hypothyroidism.

Kosher salt *is an additive-free coarse-grained salt. It is used by some Jews in the preparation of meat, as well as by gourmet cooks who prefer its texture and flavor.*

Sea salt *is the type used down through the ages and is the result of the evaporation of sea water. It comes in fine-grained or larger crystals.*

From ***Food Lover's Companion***

Triple Chocolate Cookies

3 ounces unsweetened chocolate, chopped
1 1/2 cups bittersweet chocolate chips
7 tablespoons unsalted butter, cut into pieces
2 teaspoons instant coffee granules
2 teaspoons vanilla extract
3 large eggs, room temperature
1 cup sugar
1/2 cup all-purpose flour
1/2 teaspoon baking powder
1/2 teaspoon salt
1 3/4 cups semisweet chocolate chips

Preheat oven to 350 degrees. Adjust racks to upper and lower positions. Line two large baking sheets with parchment paper.

Melt chocolates and butter in double boiler or bowl set over saucepan of simmering water, stirring frequently, until completely smooth and glossy. Cool.

Stir coffee and vanilla together until coffee is dissolved. Beat eggs and sugar in large bowl with electric mixer at medium-high speed until very thick and pale, about 4 minutes. Add coffee mixture and mix. Reduce speed to low, add chocolate mixture and mix thoroughly.

Whisk flour, baking powder and salt together. Fold flour mixture and chips into batter. Cover bowl and let stand at room temperature 20-30 minutes until batter firms up (it will appear similar to brownie batter rather than cookie dough).

Place heaping tablespoons of dough on sheets 2 inches apart. Bake until cookies are shiny and cracked on top, 11-14 minutes, rotating sheets mid way through baking. Cool cookies completely on baking sheets.

Makes 26

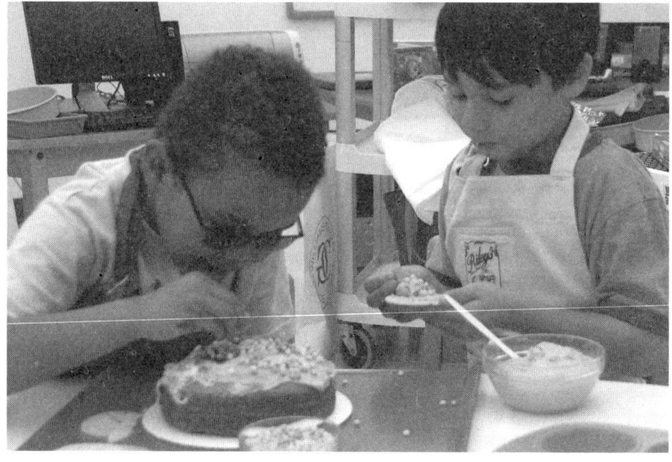

Raspberry, White Chocolate, Almond Trifle

This is a beautiful and decadent dessert for a special occasion.

- 3 1/2 cups chilled heavy whipping cream, divided
- 12 ounces high-quality white chocolate, chopped
- 1 1/4 teaspoons almond extract, divided
- 1/2 cup sugar
- 1/2 cup water
- 7 ounces crisp ladyfinger cookies
- 1 cup seedless raspberry jam, melted, divided
- 1 1/2 (12-ounce) packages frozen unsweetened raspberries, partially thawed, divided
- 1 pint container fresh raspberries
- 3/4 cup sliced almonds, toasted

Bring 1 cup cream to a simmer in medium saucepan. Remove from heat. Add white chocolate; whisk until smooth. Cool to barely lukewarm, about 10 minutes. Beat 2 1/2 cups cream and 1/2 teaspoon almond extract to soft peaks. Fold in white chocolate mixture.

Stir sugar and 1/2 cup water in small saucepan over medium heat until sugar melts. Mix in 3/4 teaspoon extract; remove syrup from heat. Quickly submerge 1 cookie in syrup; shake excess back into pan. Place dipped cookie in bottom of a 14-cup trifle dish. Repeat with enough cookies to cover bottom of dish.

Spread 1/3 of melted jam over cookies in bottom of dish. Top with 1/3 of partially thawed berries with juices. Spread 1/3 of whipped chocolate cream over berries. Repeat layering with cookies, jam, berries and cream two more times. Mound fresh berries in center of trifle. Sprinkle almonds around edge. Cover and chill at least 5 hours and up to 24 hours before serving.

Serves 16

Almond Puff

1/2 cup butter, softened
1 cup flour
2 tablespoons water
1/2 cup butter
1 cup water
1 teaspoon almond extract
1 cup flour
3 eggs

Preheat oven to 350 degrees. Cut 1/2 cup butter into 1 cup flour; sprinkle 2 tablespoons water over mixture and mix with fork. Round into ball; divide in half. On ungreased baking sheet pat each half into a strip, 12 x 3-inches, and place about 3 inches apart.

In medium saucepan heat 1/2 cup butter and 1 cup water to rolling boil. Remove from heat and quickly stir in extract and 1 cup flour. Stir vigorously over low heat until mixture forms a ball, about 1 minute. Remove from heat. Beat in eggs, all at one time, until smooth. Divide in half; spread each half evenly over strips, covering completely.

Bake 60 minutes or until topping is crisp and brown. Cool. Frost with glaze and sprinkle with nuts.

Glaze

1 1/2 cups powdered sugar
2 tablespoons butter, softened
1 1/2 teaspoons almond or vanilla extract
1-2 tablespoons warm water
1/2 cup sliced almonds, lightly toasted

Glaze: Mix sugar, butter, extract and water until smooth.

Note: When eggs are added dough may look as if something is wrong, but keep on mixing; it will all come together.

Chocolate Roll

Cake

5 eggs, separated
1 cup sugar
3 tablespoons cocoa
Cocoa and powdered sugar
1 cup heavy cream
2 tablespoons sugar

Preheat oven to 350 degrees. Beat egg yolks and sugar together 7-10 minutes or until very thick. Beat egg whites until stiff and add to sugar mixture along with cocoa.

Line an 11 x 15-inch cookie sheet with parchment paper or foil and spread mixture over this. Bake 20-25 minutes. Place cake on a damp towel or towel sprinkled with cocoa and powdered sugar. Remove paper or foil. Keep cake intact and cut off hard edges. Roll cake in towel to cool.

Whip cream until stiff, add 2 tablespoons sugar; unroll cake and cover with cream. Roll up cake using towel to keep it in shape. Wrap in towel or wax paper and place in refrigerator until served. May be made the night before serving.

Note: You may also put whipped cream over top and decorate for holidays. If frosting desired recipe follows.

Frosting

2 cups powdered sugar
2 tablespoons cocoa, heaping
4-6 tablespoons butter, softened
1 teaspoon vanilla
Coffee, optional

Mix sugar and cocoa; add butter and vanilla and mix until creamy. Add a splash of coffee if desired. Frost sides and top of roll before serving.

Quick and Easy Chocolate Mousse

1 (6-ounce) bag semisweet chocolate chips
2 eggs (Egg Beaters may be used)
3 tablespoons coffee, strong and hot
1-2 tablespoons rum
3/4 cup milk, scalded

Place all ingredients in blender. Blend at high speed 2 minutes. Pour into dessert or demitasse cups and chill. May be garnished with fruit or whipped cream.

Makes 4

Panna Cotta

Andrew Sloan, Room 39 at Mission Farms
10561 Mission Road, Leawood, Kansas

1 tablespoon gelatin
1/4 cup water
1 cup milk
5 cups heavy cream
1 cup powdered sugar
1 vanilla bean, or 2 teaspoons vanilla

Dissolve gelatin in water, set aside for 5 minutes. Scald (do not boil) milk, cream, vanilla bean and powdered sugar in a stainless steel pan. Add dissolved gelatin, stir to melt. Remove vanilla bean and pour into ramekins and chill.

Garnish with fresh fruit if desired.

Serves 6 to 8

Vanilla Maple Crème Brûlée

8 large egg yolks
1/3 cup granulated sugar
2 cups heavy cream
1/2 teaspoon maple extract
1/2 teaspoon vanilla
1/4 cup light brown sugar, packed
Fresh grated nutmeg

Preheat oven to 300 degrees. In a large bowl whisk egg yolks and sugar together until sugar is dissolved and mixture is thick and pale yellow. Whisk in cream, vanilla and maple. Strain mixture into large mixing bowl, skimming off any solids or foam. Place six 6-ounce ramekins in a baking pan with enough water to come up halfway on sides of ramekins. Divide custard into ramekins. Bake 50-60 minutes or until set around edges but still jiggly in center. Remove from oven and leave in water bath until cooled. Remove ramekins and refrigerate at least 2 hours.

When ready to serve preheat broiler or use a cooking torch. Sprinkle about 2 tablespoons brown sugar and nutmeg on top. Torch until sugar is melted or broil 2 minutes, keeping oven door open to watch as sugar will burn easily. Serve immediately.

Homemade Caramel Pecan Sauce

1/4 cup butter
2 tablespoons flour
1 1/4 cups brown sugar
3/4 cup light corn syrup
1 (5-ounce) can evaporated milk
1 1/2 cups chopped pecans, toasted
4 (1.4-ounce) toffee bars, chopped or 16 miniature Heath bars, chopped

Melt butter over low heat and add flour, stirring until smooth. Stir in sugar and corn syrup. Bring mixture to a boil, reduce heat and simmer, stirring constantly, 5 minutes. Remove from heat and cool 15 minutes. Gradually stir in milk, pecans and candy bars. Serve warm.

Heavenly Hot Fudge Sauce

1/2 cup butter
2 (1-ounce) squares semisweet chocolate
2 (1-ounce) squares unsweetened chocolate
1 (13-ounce) can evaporated milk
3 cups sugar
1/2 teaspoon salt

Melt butter and chocolate in double boiler. When melted gradually add sugar and salt. After mixing thoroughly, add milk slowly. Continue to heat until sauce is smooth and sugar is totally dissolved.

Note: Keeps well in the freezer but does not freeze solid, so spoonfuls can be easily removed.

Dessert Cheese Tray

Creamy Havarti
Brie (at room temperature)
Gouda
Fontina
Jarlsberg

Serve with fresh fruit: grapes, Bosc pears
Sweet whole Wheat Tea Biscuits

Kids' Recipes

Menu Ideas

Kids' Recipes

Chocolate Pickle Pie

What a surprise puppeteer Paul Mesner had for the Kindergarten class from CCVI. He invited them to his fanciful puppet workshop for a party and tour. They were introduced to the chef and his assistant from Sleeping Beauty's castle. It seems the Queen, who was pregnant with Sleeping Beauty, was having cravings. She ordered the chef to prepare Chocolate Pickle Pie; this became the children's treat of the day. They did eat the pie.

A good story and party atmosphere can spark the appetite.

1 (6-ounce) pre-made graham cracker pie crust
1 (.9-ounce) package instant chocolate pudding and pie filling
2 cups milk
1 (7-ounce) can Reddi-Whip Topping
Pickle slices of choice

Prepare pie filling per package directions and refrigerate. Before serving decorate with Reddi-Whip and top with pickles.

French Breakfast Puffs

1/3 cup Crisco
1/2 cup sugar
1 egg
1 1/2 cups flour
1 1/2 teaspoons baking powder
1/2 teaspoon salt
1/4 teaspoon nutmeg
1/2 cup milk
1/2 cup sugar
1 teaspoon cinnamon
1/2 cup butter, melted

Preheat oven to 350 degrees. Thoroughly mix Crisco, egg and sugar; combine dry ingredients. Grease mini muffin pans and fill 3/4 full. Bake 15 minutes. While baking, mix sugar and cinnamon. When baked, dip in butter and roll in sugar mixture.

Note: These can be frozen, reheated in microwave and served warm. Recipe can be easily doubled or tripled.

Muffin Tin Egg Sandwiches

1/4 cup milk
3 eggs
6 cooked sausage patties
6 cheese slices
6 cooked biscuits

Preheat oven to 350 degrees. Stir eggs and milk together. Fill 6 muffin tins with egg mixture. Bake 20-25 minutes. Cut biscuits in half. Place egg, cheese and sausage between biscuit halves.

Breakfast Pizza

4-6 eggs
1/2 pound sausage or other breakfast meat, cooked
2 cups shredded cheese, any kind
Pre-made pizza dough

Preheat oven to 350 degrees. Whip eggs in a bowl with a little water. Add cooked meat to egg mixture. Mix in cheese (you do not need to use all). Spread pizza dough on a cookie sheet or pizza pan. Make a small "lip" around the edge of dough so mix doesn't run off. Gently pour egg, meat and cheese mix onto dough. Bake approximately 25 minutes. Dough should be done and eggs thoroughly cooked.

Breakfast Treats

These are very crispy and can take the place of a sweet roll.

1 package original Crescent Roll dough
2/3 cup butter, softened
2/3 cup light brown sugar
1 1/2 cups chopped or broken pecans

Preheat oven to 375 degrees. Unroll dough in a whole sheet. Place dough on a jelly roll pan and carefully stretch, press and push dough to edges of pan. Combine butter and sugar in a saucepan and bring to a boil. Boil one minute, stirring constantly. Pour hot mixture over dough and with the back of a spoon spread syrup over all the dough. Cover with pecans.

Bake 14-18 minutes. Let cool and cut diagonally from side to side of pan. Should make 40-50 pieces.

Granola, Fruit and Yogurt Parfait

Granola

1/2 cup canola oil
1/3 cup hot water
2/3 cup honey
6 cups rolled oats
3/4 cup sliced almonds
3/4 cup chopped pecans
3/4 cup chopped walnuts

Preheat oven to 325 degrees, position racks in upper and lower thirds of oven. In a medium bowl, whisk together oil, hot water and honey. In a large bowl, stir together oats, almonds, pecans and walnuts. Pour honey mixture into oat mixture and stir until oats and nuts are evenly coated. Spread granola in a single layer onto baking sheets. May need to do more than one baking.

Bake 15 minutes, stir, and switch the position of the pans. Bake 15 more minutes, or until toasted. Allow granola to cool completely. Do not overbake. Granola will harden as it cools. Break apart any large lumps and store in an airtight container at room temperature for several weeks.

For two parfaits use 1/2 cup of each: homemade granola, cut up fruit (such as kiwi, strawberries, blueberries and peaches) and plain yogurt. Flavor yogurt with maple syrup, honey, orange juice or other flavoring to taste. In a parfait glass, alternate layers of yogurt mixture, homemade granola and fresh fruit.

Oatmeal Breakfast Bars

4 cups quick cooking oats
1 cup packed brown sugar
1 teaspoon salt
1 1/2 cups chopped walnuts
1 cup flaked coconut
3/4 cup melted butter
3/4 cup orange marmalade

Preheat oven to 425 degrees. In a mixing bowl, combine oats, brown sugar and salt. Stir in remaining ingredients and mix well. Press into a greased 15 x 10-inch baking pan. Bake 15 to 17 minutes or until golden brown. Cool on a wire rack.

Note: Raisins or cranraisins can be substituted for the nuts.

Makes about 30

Oh, Nuts! Granola

3 cups old-fashioned rolled oats
1 cup pecan halves, roughly chopped
2 teaspoons ground cinnamon
1/4 teaspoon kosher salt
1/2 cup packed light brown sugar
1/4 cup water
2 tablespoons canola oil
1 tablespoon pure vanilla extract

Preheat oven to 300 degrees, position racks in the upper and lower thirds of oven. Spray two rimmed baking sheets with cooking spray. In a large bowl, mix oats, pecans, cinnamon and salt. In a small saucepan, combine brown sugar and water. Bring to a simmer over medium heat, stirring until the sugar is melted. Stir in oil and vanilla. Pour over oat mixture and stir until well mixed.

Divide mixture between the two baking sheets and spread evenly. Bake 15 minutes, stir granola, and switch the positions of the pans. Bake until oats are golden brown and nuts look well toasted, another 10-15 minutes. Oats may feel soft but will crisp as they cool. Let cool completely in pans.

Yields 4 to 5 cups.

Note: The looser texture of this granola makes it perfect for sprinkling over a bowl of yogurt.

Green Eggs and Ham

You have read the book, now prepare the feast.

1/4 teaspoon green food color
5 tablespoons water
Sliced ham
2 eggs

Mix food color and water, set aside. Separate egg white from egg yolks. Add 2 teaspoons food color to egg whites and mix; add 2 tablespoons colored mixture to egg yolks. Brush ham with color mixture and fry until cooked; remove from pan. Add egg whites to pan and cook until they start to set. Place egg yolks on top of egg whites. Add an additional teaspoon of color mixture to help steam eggs. Cover fry pan and finish steaming eggs until done.

If you prefer scrambled eggs, add two teaspoons food color mixture to eggs and scramble. Cook scrambled eggs on medium heat, stirring until done.

Swiss-Style Muesli

1 cup milk
1/2 cup plain yogurt
1/4 cup whipping cream or milk
1/4-1/3 cup honey
1 1/2 cups muesli
2 medium bananas, thinly sliced
1 apple, finely chopped
Fresh berries such as raspberries, blueberries, blackberries or strawberries

Combine milk, yogurt, cream and honey. Stir until well combined, add muesli. Cover and chill overnight or up to 3 days. To serve, divide banana slices among 4 serving bowls. Top with muesli mix and add chopped apple and berries.

Makes 4 servings

Apple Rolls

1 (8-ounce) tube crescent rolls
1-2 apples, finely chopped
Smooth peanut butter
Cinnamon

Preheat oven to 350 degrees. Unfold crescent rolls and spread peanut butter over each. Spread apple pieces over peanut butter. Sprinkle cinnamon on top. Roll dough back into crescent shapes starting from larger end. Bake on cookie sheet 15 minutes..

Makes 8

Banana Dippers

Bananas, peeled
1 (8-ounce) bag chocolate chips
Cinnamon sugar
Peanut butter
Chopped nuts
Coconut
Ice cream sprinkles
Crushed cookies

Slice bananas into several pieces. Place chocolate chips in a microwave safe bowl and cook on high until melted, about 1 minute. Stir every 30 seconds until smooth. Dip banana slices in chocolate and roll in other ingredients as desired.

Frozen Bananas

3 bananas
6 ice-cream sticks
2 (1 1/2-ounce) chocolate bars
1 tablespoon chopped nuts, crispy rice cereal or granola

Peel bananas and remove any stringy fibers. Cut bananas in half, widthwise, and push an ice-cream stick through cut end of each half. Cover in plastic wrap and freeze about 3 hours. Place chocolate bars in a microwave-safe bowl and cook on high about 2 minutes or until chocolate melts. Check after one minute. Stir in nuts and/or cereal. Using a butter knife, spread chocolate mixture over frozen bananas to coat completely. Rest pops on a plate covered with waxed paper and freeze until ready to serve.

Makes 6 pops

Strawberry-Orange-Vanilla Smoothie

Non-Dairy Breakfast Smoothie

8 frozen strawberries
1/4 pound plain silken tofu
1/3 cup orange juice
2 tablespoons honey
1/2 teaspoon pure vanilla

Combine all ingredients in a blender and blend until smooth.

Serves 1

Low Calorie Pumpkin Dip

3/4 cup 1/3 less-fat cream cheese, softened
1/2 cup packed brown sugar
1/2 cup canned pumpkin
2 teaspoons maple syrup
1/2 teaspoon cinnamon
24 apple slices

Place first three ingredients in a medium bowl and beat with mixer at medium speed until well blended. Add syrup and cinnamon and beat until smooth. Cover and chill for 30 minutes. Serve with apple slices.

Note: Dip apple slices in pineapple juice or Sprite to keep them from turning brown.

Melt-in-Your-Mouth Melon

1 small honeydew melon
Raspberry sorbet
Chocolate chips

Halve honeydew, discard seeds and chill overnight. The next day, freeze halves for 15 minutes. Remove from freezer and pack with sorbet, gently leveling top. Using a chilled knife, slice each half into half and into halves again (make sure melon is sorbet side up). Finally, insert a row of chocolate chips as "seeds" and serve immediately.

Berry Ice Cubes and Lemonade

1 (11.5-ounce) can frozen concentrate berry mix juice
24 raspberries or 8 strawberries, sliced
2 quarts water
1 1/3 cups sugar (or more to taste)
1 1/3 cups fresh lemon juice
8 lemon slices, optional
8 mint sprigs, optional

Pour juice concentrate and 1 can water into a pitcher. Mix to combine and pour juice into two ice cube trays, adding raspberries or sliced strawberries. Freeze. Combine remaining water and sugar in a medium saucepan. Bring to a boil and stir to combine. Reduce to simmer and cook until sugar is dissolved, about 1 to 2 minutes. Remove from heat. Strain lemon juice and add to sugar syrup. Chill. Slit each lemon slice, if using, once, from center to rind, then press slits onto eight glasses. Fill each glass with 3 berry ice cubes and lemonade. Garnish with mint.

Fruity Kebobs

It is a known fact that putting food on a stick improves the flavor.

1 large red apple, cut into 8 wedges
6 marshmallows
1 small jar creamy peanut butter
1 large banana, cut into1-inch slices
2 skewers

Carefully push a skewer through ingredients, starting with apple, then a marshmallow, then banana. Spread a dollop of peanut butter on top of marshmallow. Alternate ingredients until half used. Repeat with second skewer.

Ladybugs on a Stick

Red grapes
Small wooden skewers
Strawberries
Mini chocolate chips
Honeydew melon

Push half of a red grape onto skewer for the head. Next, push on a hulled strawberry body and score the back to create wings. For spots, use a toothpick to gently press mini chocolate chips, tips down, into the fruit. Arrange skewers on a sliced honeydew melon half.

Strawberry Sparkles

1 pint fresh strawberries
1/4 cup colored sugar
1 (4-ounce) package cream cheese, softened
2 teaspoons confectioners sugar
4 teaspoons milk
1/2 teaspoon vanilla

Wash whole berries and pat them dry with a paper towel. Fill a shallow bowl with colored sugar. In a separate bowl, blend cream cheese, sugar, milk and vanilla with a fork until smooth and creamy. Add more milk if needed to achieve desired consistency. Holding berries by their stems, dip into cheese mixture, roll in sugar and enjoy.

Strawberry Mice

Fresh strawberries
Mini chocolate chips
Black decorator's icing
Almond slivers
Toothpick
Red lace licorice
Wedges of cheese, your choice

For each mouse, slice a small section from the side of a strawberry so it sits flat. Press a mini chocolate chip onto tip of strawberry for a nose, using a small dab of icing to secure it in place if needed. Add icing eyes and stick 2 almond slivers onto top of berry for ears. For a tail, use a toothpick to carve a small hole in the back of berry and push end of a piece of licorice lace into hole. Serve these cute treats with small triangles of cheese.

Watermelon Stars

Watermelon
Popsicle sticks
Star-shaped cookie cutter, your choice of size

Cut star shapes from 1-inch-thick slices of seedless watermelon. Insert a stick into each star, set stars on an aluminum foil-lined baking sheet. Cover with another sheet of foil and freeze for 1 hour or until firm.

Popcorn Balls

3 batches popped popcorn
1 (10-ounce) bag mini marshmallows
8 tablespoons butter, melted
Large brown paper bag
Butter

Place popcorn in bag. Melt marshmallows and butter together in microwave. Pour mixture over popcorn. Mix well with a wooden spoon. Butter hands and pack popcorn together in balls. If too loose, let cool a couple minutes and retry. Wrap in plastic wrap or zip lock bags.

Note: Works best to fold down sides of paper bag.

Mexicali Popcorn

10 cups popped popcorn, warm
1 tablespoon taco seasoning
1/4 cup melted butter
1/4 cup grated Cheddar or Colby cheese

Place popcorn in a large bowl. In a small bowl, mix seasoning with butter. Add grated cheese, stir into warm popcorn.

Popcorn Mix

Prepared by an adult with child's help.

9-10 cups oven-toasted corn cereal squares
5 cups popped popcorn
1 1/2 cups (7-ounces) slivered almonds
1 cup light brown sugar, packed
1/2 cup butter
1/2 cup light corn syrup
1 teaspoon vanilla extract
1/2 teaspoon baking soda
1 2/3 cups (10-ounce) packages swirled milk chocolate and caramel morsels
1 (6-ounce) package sweetened dried cranberries

Preheat oven to 250 degrees. Grease large roasting pan. Mix cereal, popcorn and nuts in roasting pan. Combine brown sugar, butter and corn syrup in a medium saucepan. Bring to a boil over medium heat, stirring constantly. Boil, stir occasionally, 5 minutes. Remove from heat, stir in vanilla and baking soda (this will foam up). Pour evenly over cereal mixture and stir to coat evenly. Bake 45 minutes, stirring every 15 minutes. Cool in pan, stirring frequently to break apart mixture. Stir in morsels and cranberries. Store in an airtight container.

Halloween Party Mix

Prepared by an adult with child's help.

1 (11-ounce) package small pretzels
1 (10 1/2-ounce) package peanut butter Ritz Bits
1 cup dry roasted peanuts
1 cup sugar
1/2 cup butter
1/2 cup light corn syrup
2 tablespoons vanilla
1 teaspoon baking soda
1 (10-ounce) package M & M's
1 (18-ounce) package candy corn

Preheat oven to 250 degrees. Combine pretzels, crackers and peanuts in a large bowl. In a large saucepan combine sugar, butter and corn syrup. Bring to a boil over medium heat and boil 5 minutes, stirring to prevent sticking. Remove from heat and stir in vanilla and baking soda, (this will foam up). Pour over pretzel mixture and stir until coated. Spread onto a greased 15" x 10" x 1" pan. Bake 45 minutes, stirring every 10-15 minutes. Break apart while warm. Toss with M & M's and candy corn. Cool completely and store in airtight container.

Makes 16 cups

Popcorn Salad

Good for "big people" too. Very unusual.

- 2 cups finely chopped celery
- 1/2 cup finely chopped red onion
- 3 (8-ounce) cans water chestnuts
- 1 1/2 cups shredded Cheddar cheese
- 1/2 pound bacon, cooked and crumbled
- 2 cups mayonnaise
- 2/3 cup sugar
- 1 teaspoon vinegar
- 16 cups popped popcorn

Mix first 5 ingredients. In separate bowl mix next 3 ingredients. Combine the mixtures. Just before serving add popcorn and gently mix in.

Hummus

Paul Mesner, Puppeteer
Paul says kids love this mild version.

- 2-6 tablespoons hot water
- 1 large clove garlic, peeled
- 1 (15-ounce) can garbanzo beans, drained and rinsed
- 2 tablespoons tahini (sesame paste)
- Juice of 1-2 lemons
- 2-6 tablespoons olive oil
- 1 teaspoon cumin
- 1/2 teaspoon salt, or to taste
- Pine nuts, toasted in olive oil
- Chopped parsley (optional)
- Paprika (optional)

Cut garlic clove in half and soak in boiling water 5 minutes. In food processor or blender add tahini, lemon juice, 2 tablespoons olive oil, cumin and blanched garlic, pulse 3 times, add beans and pulse three times. Pulse or stir, adding more oil, hot water and lemon juice until smooth and creamy. To serve sprinkle pine nuts, paprika and parsley on top, then drizzle with olive oil, or serve plain.

Note: Serve with toasted pita bread wedges.

Zucchini Oven Chips

A healthy alternative to potato chips.

1/4 cup dry breadcrumbs
1/4 cup (1-ounce) grated fresh Parmesan cheese
1/4 teaspoon seasoned salt
1/4 teaspoon garlic powder
1/8 teaspoon freshly ground black pepper
2 tablespoons fat-free milk
2 1/2 cups (1/4-inch-thick) slices of zucchini (about 2 small)
Cooking spray

Preheat oven to 425 degrees. Combine first 5 ingredients in a medium bowl, stirring with a whisk. Pour milk into a shallow bowl. Dip zucchini in milk and dredge in breadcrumb mixture. Place coated slices on an ovenproof wire rack coated with cooking spray; place rack on a baking sheet. Bake 30 minutes or until browned and crisp. Serve immediately.

Note: Dip chips in Italian tomato sauce or sauce of your choice. Other squash may be substituted for zucchini.

Serves 4

Chicken Nuggets with Mustard Dipping Sauce

1/2 cup low-fat buttermilk
1 1/2 pounds skinless, boneless, chicken breasts, cut into large bite-sized pieces
4 cups cornflakes
1 teaspoon paprika
1/2 teaspoon sugar
1/4 teaspoon salt
Cooking spray

Sauce:
1/2 cup prepared mustard
1/4 cup honey
1/2 teaspoon peeled grated ginger

Combine buttermilk and chicken, marinate in refrigerator 30 minutes, drain.

Preheat oven to 375 degrees.

Place cornflakes, paprika, sugar and salt in food processor; process until cornflakes are finely chopped. Combine chicken and cornflake mixture, tossing well to coat. Place chicken on a baking sheet covered with cooking spray. Bake 15 minutes or until chicken is cooked through.

To prepare sauce combine mustard, honey and ginger. Serve with chicken.

Serves 8

Pinwheels

1 teaspoon cinnamon
1 tablespoon sugar
2 (6-inch) flour tortillas
2 tablespoons melted butter

Preheat oven to 350 degrees. Brush a small baking sheet with butter. Combine cinnamon and sugar in small bowl. Brush each tortilla with melted butter and spread half the cinnamon and sugar mixture over each. Roll up tortillas jelly roll fashion and place seam side down on baking sheet. Brush tops and sides with butter. Bake 8-10 minutes. Cool rolls and slice into 1/2-inch pieces.

Serves 2

Cheese Stars

Great for the 4th of July.

5 (10-inch) flour tortillas
Sliced cheese (Cheddar, provolone or mozzarella)
Chili powder or paprika
2 Star-shaped cookie cutters (one about 4" the other about 2")

Preheat oven to 350 degrees. Use larger cookie cutter to cut stars from tortillas. Use a rolling pin to help push cutter into tortilla. Bake stars on a foil-covered cookie sheet 5 minutes.

With smaller cutter cut out an equal number of cheese stars and place atop tortilla stars. Bake stars 2 more minutes or until cheese melts.

Sprinkle stars with chili powder or paprika and let cool before serving.

Green Tortilla Chips

You can use whatever color suits your fancy—or holiday.

1 washable table covering
1 tablespoon green food color
1/4 cup water
(5 1/2-inch) white corn tortilla shells

Mix food color and water. Brush color on both sides of a 5 1/2" white corn tortilla with a pastry brush. Let dry for one hour. Slice into triangles and fry in hot vegetable oil. Drain shells on paper towels, salt to taste. These can be baked in a 350 degree oven until crisp, about 10 minutes, but color will not be as strong.

Note: Enough coloring for approximately 40 shells.

Leprechaun Legs

1 (8-ounce) package cream cheese, room temperature
1 (8-ounce) can crushed pineapple, drained
Celery, cleaned and trimmed
Green food coloring

Whip cream cheese until soft and fluffy. Blend pineapple and cream cheese until completely mixed together. Add food coloring to desired shade. Cut celery into pieces. Fill celery with cream cheese mixture and place on serving tray, cover and chill until ready to serve. Food coloring can be omitted.

Tasty Caterpillar

1 (8-ounce) roll pizza dough, or (6.5-ounce) packaged mix
2 white button mushrooms, sliced
Olive oil for brushing
Toppings, such as peppers, carrots, olives, basil and pepperoni
Sauce of your choice
Mozzarella cheese (cut deli-style slices into disks with a biscuit cutter)

Preheat oven to 400 degrees. Lay a piece of parchment paper on a cookie sheet so that it extends slightly beyond each end. If needed, let dough rise according to package directions. Divide dough into 15 1-inch balls and combine 3 balls to make the head. Have child dust hands with flour, then arrange balls on cookie sheet and flatten slightly with palm of hand. Press mushroom slices under dough for legs. Brush dough and mushrooms with olive oil, bake until dough is starting to crisp around the edges, about 10 minutes. While dough bakes, create caterpillar features from your choice of toppings. Remove cookie sheet from oven. Using parchment paper as a carrier, lift caterpillar off cookie sheet and set it on a wire rack. When cool enough to touch, let child paint surface with sauce and arrange cheese and toppings. Again, using the parchment, set caterpillar back on the cookie sheet and bake until cheese is just starting to brown, about 8 minutes. Let cool slightly, slice and serve.

Pretzels

- 2 packages yeast
- 2 cups warm water
- 1/2 cup sugar
- 2 teaspoons salt
- 1/4 cup butter, softened
- 2 eggs
- 6 1/2 cups unsifted flour
- Coarse salt

Place water in a large mixing bowl, sprinkle with yeast and stir until dissolved. Add sugar, salt, butter, 1 egg and 3 cups flour. Beat until smooth. Add enough additional flour to make a stiff dough. Cover tightly with aluminum foil. Refrigerate 2 – 24 hours.

Preheat oven to 400 degrees. Turn out onto a lightly floured surface. Allow to warm slightly. Divide dough in half and divide each half into at least 16 pieces. Have children roll dough between both hands into about 10-inch long pencil shapes and form these however they would like; place on a lightly greased baking sheet. Mix together 1 egg and 2 tablespoon water. Brush over pretzels and sprinkle with coarse salt. Let rise until double. Bake about 15 minutes.

Chocolate Mountain Cookies

- 4 ounces unsweetened chocolate, melted and cooled
- 1/4 cup butter
- 2 cups sugar
- 4 eggs
- 1/2 cup nuts, chopped
- 1 teaspoon baking powder
- 2 cups flour
- 1/2 teaspoon salt
- Powdered sugar

Preheat oven to 300 degrees. Cream together chocolate, butter and sugar. Add eggs, one at a time, beating after each addition. Add remaining ingredients and mix well. Refrigerate 20 minutes. Form into balls and roll in powdered sugar. Place on greased cookie sheet and bake 15-20 minutes.

Cookies on a Stick

- 1 package sugar cookie mix
- Craft sticks
- Cookie cutters of your choice
- Ready to spread frosting
- Food coloring
- Assorted sprinkles

Prepare cookie dough according to instructions. Roll dough on a floured surface about 1/4-inch thick. Cut with shaped cutter. Carefully insert a wooden stick 2 inches into bottom part of shape. Carefully smooth dough on both sides of stick. The wooden stick should not protrude from cookies. Place cookies on a greased baking sheet in a preheated oven and bake according to package instructions. When cookies are completely cool decorate as desired.

A Cool Treat

- 11 ice cream sandwich bars (Blue Bell recommended)
- 1 (16-ounce) container Cool Whip
- 1 (10-ounce) Heath Bar Toffee Bits

Line a 9 x 13-inch pan with sandwiches (cut to totally fill pan). Mix Cool Whip with toffee bits and cover sandwiches. Return to freezer. Thaw 5-10 minutes before cutting into serving pieces.

Note: May add nuts or strawberries.

Kid's Crafts

Fingerprint Flowers and Fruits

Fabric Paint, assorted colors
Tempera Paint, assorted colors
Fabric
Paper suitable for cards, envelopes
Permanent marker

This is a great way to make your own greeting cards or invitations. Be sure to practice on scrap paper before using the final paper or cloth.

Flowers: For each petal press your paint-covered index finger against the paper or cloth and roll from side to side. Add small dots of paint to the center with your pinkie. Add a stem if you wish.

Apple: Make two side-by-side overlapping prints with your index finger. Draw a marker stem and add a pinkie-print leaf.

Pear: With index finger make two overlapping perpendicular prints. Draw a marker stem and add a pinkie-print leaf. Once pear is dry, add a marker dot to bottom of the pear.

Orange: Make a large circle with the tip of your index finger. Add a marker stem and add a pinkie-print leaf. Once dry, draw a star on the bottom.

Cherries: Make circles with the tip of index finger, then draw marker stems. Once dry, add marker dots on the bottom of the cherries.

Leaf Print Eggs

Small flat leaves (fern, cilantro, dill, thyme, mint)
Hard-boiled white eggs
Nylon stockings, cut in 3" sections
Rubber bands
Water
White vinegar
Food coloring
Large glasses or small bowl
Spoon

Lay leaf on egg. If needed, dampen egg slightly to help hold it on. Cover egg with a section of stocking to hold in place. Pull together each end of the stocking and secure ends with rubber bands.

For each dye bath, mix 1/2 cup warm water, 1 teaspoon vinegar and 10-20 drops of food coloring in a glass. (You can use commercial egg dye.) Carefully submerge the nylon-wrapped egg in bath and let it soak about 4 minutes. Use a slotted spoon to remove egg from bath and set it on a covered work surface. Carefully remove rubber bands, nylon and leaf. Allow egg to dry completely before handling it further.

Mold an Ice Candle

This is really not suitable for young children. Be very careful with melted wax.

Scissors
Round cardboard container
(from salt or oatmeal)
Paper towel
Cooking oil
Knife
White tapered candle
Large tin can
1 pound paraffin wax
Large saucepan
Wooden skewer
Crayon pieces
Large spoon
Crushed ice
Bowl

Prepare mold by cutting off top of cardboard container. Use a paper towel to coat the inside of container with cooking oil. Trim bottom from taper so it is the same height as mold.

Fill tin can with wax. Place it in a saucepan filled with 2 inches of water and set pan over low heat. Use a wooden skewer to stir the melting wax. Mix in crayon pieces to get your desired candle color.

Pour 1/2 inch of wax into prepared mold and immediately stick taper into the center, wick end up. Hold taper in place for a minute or two while the wax sets. Spoon 2 inches of crushed ice around taper, then cover ice almost completely with melted wax. Add more ice, then more wax, alternating until mold is filled.

Set mold in a bowl for about an hour (it will leak water), letting wax harden completely. Peel off cardboard.

Quick Decorated Pumpkins

Small clean pumpkins, orange or white
Newspapers
Rubber stamps
Black ink pad
Small paint brush
Glue
Glitter
Ribbon

Stamps come in so many different ways now, choose what you want to say: "boo," child's name or whatever you wish. Cover work surface with paper. Apply inked stamp to pumpkin. Allow to dry. Paint glue over stamps and dust with glitter. Shake excess glue onto paper. Tie ribbon around stem.

Halloween Greetings

Clean pumpkin
Small paint brush
Letters from alphabet cereal or macaroni pasta
Metallic paint
Glue

Apply a thin line of glue where you want letters. Place letters accordingly and allow glue to dry. Color letters by painting only top surfaces with a small amount of metallic paint. Use paint to add embellishments between words and/or stem.

Painting a Pumpkin

Acrylic Paint: navy blue, white, red iron oxide
Black permanent marker, fine point
Ball point pen
Photo
Paint brush
Clear acrylic gloss spray
Raffia and artificial leaves
Hot glue gun
Pumpkins: pie pumpkins are easiest

Photos by Gene Schmidt

Draw your idea with pen and then paint with appropriate colors. Let paint dry, coat with acrylic spray. Decorate with raffia and glue leaves.

Sugar-Cone Cornucopia

Sugar ice cream cones
Store-bought decorator's icing
Doilies, optional
Ribbon
Fruit-shaped candies or cereal

Tie a ribbon around the opening of a cone. With a tube of decorator's icing print name of each person along the side of the cone. Place cone on a doily-covered saucer. Fill with candies such as raspberry jellies, fruit-shaped sweets, marzipan fruits, candy corn and citrus slices. For an inexpensive alternative, use fruit-shaped cereal. Let goodies spill out over opening and around cone.

Child's Art Work

1 box announcement cards (size 6 bar)
Matching envelopes
Glue stick
Photos or artwork cut to 3 1/2 x 5-inches

A child's art can make great note cards. Scan art into your computer or onto a disk. Chose to either print using home computer and printer or take disk to a camera store that prints digital. Have multiple copies made into 3 1/2 x 5-inches photos, matte or glossy. Glue stick a photo to front of card and write message on inside. If same message is desired for multiple cards run them through your computer printer.

Shaving Cream Art

1 can unscented shaving cream
Assorted play dishes, utensils, plastic spoons, knives, etc.
Kitchen table or play table that is waterproof

Spray shaving cream on table top. (Shaving cream is basically foaming soap and should not harm most surfaces). Spray in mounds or in a plastic bowl. Let children pretend they are making ice cream, cookies, pies and cakes. Can wipe a thin layer and allow children to finger paint with it or just write or draw. For little ones a high chair with a tray is great, will keep them entertained for an hour.

Adult supervision is necessary. This is a "clean" project and will not harm clothing.

Tip
When you get a splinter, reach for the scotch tape before the tweezers or a needle. Simply put the scotch tape over the splinter and pull it off. Scotch tape removes most splinters painlessly and easily.

Steering Committee

Chairman Sally Cobb

Advisor Mary Jo Truog

Appetizers
Tracy Miller & Nan McConnell

Breakfast & Brunch
Courtney Earnest, Ashley Pindell & Corinne McCanse

Soup and Salad
Mary Ann Wilson & Barbara Mura

Breads
Carol Spachman

Sides
Kristi Shaffer

Entrees
Susan Truog & Janice McCollum

Desserts
Erma Peterson & Debbie Frazee

Kids
Peggy Schmidt

Testers

Pat Calliham
Kathy Cirino
Sally Cobb
Jennifer Coen
Linda Cook
Una Creditor
Virginia Crosby
Diana Cusser
Martha Dooley
Judy Donnelly
Courtney Ernest
Emily Eckels
Barbara Eiszner
Jenny Erdman
Debbie Frazee
Lora Manka Garrison
Judy Glynn
Kendall Goff
Tess Hawes
Birgitta Heikel
Lynn Hindley
Anya Holmes
Barbara Joslin
Cynthia Lynders
Nan McConnell
Corinne McCanse
Janice McCollum
Tracy Miller
Katie Moreland
Barbara Mura
Donna Nally
Marsha O'Connor
Erma Peterson
Ashley Pindell
Kathy Rapley
Karen Roberts
Peggy Schmidt
Kristi Shaffer
Kathy Shaffer
Nan Streen
Michele Stowers
Erin Tate
B J Thornburg
Mary Ann Toohey
Mary Jo Truog
Susan Truog
Bobbie Vanice
Mary Ann Wilson

Contributors

Todd Achepohl
Diane Barker
Gerry Barker
Benedict Builders Farm
Kris Bethay
Nancy Bethay
Doris Boyd
Bread of Life Bakery
Connie Brouillette
Laura Brown
Beverly Bryson
Pat Calliham
Cathy Campbell
Kathy Cirino
Elaine Claiborne
Sandra Clay
Sally Cobb
Jennifer Coen
Linda Cook
Ricki Creamer
Una Creditor
Virginia Crosby
Diana Cusser
Enid Dickson
Dawn Dinneen
Judy Donnelly
Martha Dooley
Mary Lee Duff
Courtney Earnest
Emily Eckels
Barbara Eiszner
Jill Eliason
Jane Emley
Jenny Erdman
Lynette Ewy
Jenny Ferguson
Jim Fields
Sharon Fields
Jim Fitterling
Debbie Frazee
Karla Fredericks
Mark Fredericks
Lora Manka Garrison
Barbara Gattermeir
Judy Glynn
Kendall Dittmer Goff
Green Dirt Farms
Barbara Haggerty
Karen Hall
Amy Hardy
Tess Hawes
Jo Hayes
Birgitta Heikel
Susan Herbert
Lynn Hindley
Marilyn Hodges
Carolyn Holder
Anya Holmes
Louise Howe
Ann Joiner
Peggy Jones
Barbara Joslin
Katie Kennedy
Ann Kindred
Jennifer Krause
Cynthia Lackner
Bob LaDue
Marilyn Lakee
Leslie Laskey
Carrie LaVoy
Heather Holder Leech
Kimberly LeValley
Cynthia Lynders
Amanda Martens
Elizabeth Mayer
Margaret Mayer
Susan F. Mayerle
Michelle McBrayer
Corinne McCanse
Janice McCollum
Nan McConnell
Annie O'Mara McCormick
Thomas McCoy
April McCracken
Louise Meyers
Judy Miller
Tracy Miller
Kay Moffat
Janell Moore
Maggie Moore
Katie Moreland
Holly Mosher
Brenda Munden
Barbara Mura
Donna Nally
Janise Naughton
Pat Nelson
Margaret Nerman
Debbie Niemann
Harolyn O'Brien
Marsha O'Connor
Patty O'Donnell
Gloria O'Malley
Stephanie O'Marison
Sophie Pageard
Erma Peterson
Lana Peterson
Barbara Phelps
Ashley Pindell
Jim Pittman
Sally Pollock
Jan Ramirez
Patty Ramsour
Kathy Rapley
Sandra Riley
Karen Roberts
Marilyn Rue
Peggy Schmidt
Audrey Schwegler
Dan Schwimmer
Rhonda Sexton
Kathy Shaffer
Kristi Shaffer
Carol Spachman
Bill Stalder
Kim Stephens
Jodie Stockwell
Michele Stowers
Nan Streen
Helen Taliaferro
Erin Tate
Penny Tate
B. J. Thornburg
Carmen Thum
Mary Ann Toohey
Karen Trischler
Mary Jo Truog
Susan Truog
Bobbie Vanice
Gail Ward
Faye Werner
Kathleen Wilkes
Christina Wilson
Mary Ann Wilson
Ann Wissman

We regret the omission of any contributors

INDEX

A

B

Breakfasts, Brunches & Breads *(continued)*

Broccoli

C

Cabbage

Carrots

Cheese

Cheese *(continued)*

Cherries

Chicken

Chocolate

Coconut

Cookies and Bars

Entrees *(continued)*

F

Fish

Frosting

G

Grapes

Grilling Recipes

Grits

K

Kids' Crafts

Kids' Recipes

Kids' Recipes *(continued)*

L

Lamb

Leeks

M

Mangoes

Mushrooms

N

Nuts

Nuts *(continued)*

O

Onions

R

S

Seafood

Side Dishes

Soups

Spinach

Squash *(also see Zucchini)*

Strawberries

V

Z

A Taste of Kansas City II ...Menus and More

The Children's Center for the Visually Impaired
3101 Main Street
Kansas City, Missouri 64111
816-841-CCVI • Fax:816-753-7836
www.ccvi.org

Please send _______ copy(ies)	@ $25.00 each $ _____________
Shipping and handling for first book	@ $ 6.00 each $ _____________
Shipping and handling for each additional book to same address	@ $ 3.00 each $ _____________
	TOTAL $ _____________

Name ____

Address ____

City ______________________ State_______ Zip ______________

Phone ____________________ Cell Phone ____________________

Payment: ❑ Check ❑ Visa ❑ MasterCard ❑ American Express

Card Number ______________ SIC Number _________ Expiration Date _________

Signature __________________________________

Make checks payable to *Friends of CCVI.*

A Taste of Kansas City II ...Menus and More

The Children's Center for the Visually Impaired
3101 Main Street
Kansas City, Missouri 64111
816-841-CCVI • Fax:816-753-7836
www.ccvi.org

Please send _______ copy(ies)	@ $25.00 each $ _____________
Shipping and handling for first book	@ $ 6.00 each $ _____________
Shipping and handling for each additional book to same address	@ $ 3.00 each $ _____________
	TOTAL $ _____________

Name ____

Address ____

City ______________________ State_______ Zip ______________

Phone ____________________ Cell Phone ____________________

Payment: ❑ Check ❑ Visa ❑ MasterCard ❑ American Express

Card Number ______________ SIC Number _________ Expiration Date _________

Signature __________________________________

Make checks payable to *Friends of CCVI.*

A Taste of Kansas City ...Then and Now
and
A Taste of Kansas City II ...Menus and More

The Children's Center for the Visually Impaired
3101 Main Street, Kansas City, Missouri 64111
816-841-CCVI • Fax:816-753-7836 • www.ccvi.org

Please send ______set(s) of two books	@ $40.00	$______
Shipping and handling for one set of two books	@ $ 9.00	$______
Shipping and handling for each additional set of two books to same address	@ $ 5.00	$______
	TOTAL	$______

Name ____
Address ____
City ______________________ State______ Zip ____________
Phone ________________ Cell Phone ________________
Payment: ❑ Check ❑ Visa ❑ MasterCard ❑ American Express
Card Number ____________ SIC Number ________ Expiration Date ________

Signature ______________________________

Make checks payable to *Friends of CCVI.*

— — — — — — — — — — — — — — —

A Taste of Kansas City ...Then and Now
and
A Taste of Kansas City II ...Menus and More

The Children's Center for the Visually Impaired
3101 Main Street, Kansas City, Missouri 64111
816-841-CCVI • Fax:816-753-7836 • www.ccvi.org

Please send ______set(s) of two books	@ $40.00	$______
Shipping and handling for one set of two books	@ $ 9.00	$______
Shipping and handling for each additional set of two books to same address	@ $ 5.00	$______
	TOTAL	$______

Name ____
Address ____
City ______________________ State______ Zip ____________
Phone ________________ Cell Phone ________________
Payment: ❑ Check ❑ Visa ❑ MasterCard ❑ American Express
Card Number ____________ SIC Number ________ Expiration Date ________

Signature ______________________________

Make checks payable to *Friends of CCVI.*